JOHNS HOPKINS UNIVERSITY STUDIES

IN

HISTORICAL AND POLITICAL SCIENCE

———————

EXTRA VOLUMES   NEW SERIES, No. 10

SLAVERY AGITATION IN VIRGINIA 1829-1832

SLAVERY AGITATION IN VIRGINIA 1829-1832

Awarded the Mrs. Simon Baruch University
Prize for 1929

BY

THEODORE M. WHITFIELD, Ph.D.

BALTIMORE: THE JOHNS HOPKINS PRESS
LONDON: HUMPHREY MILFORD
OXFORD UNIVERSITY PRESS

1930

To My Father
James Morehead Whitfield
and My Aunt
Emma Morehead Whitfield

PREFACE

During the fourth decade of the nineteenth century Virginia's attitude towards slavery underwent a profound change. The negro had long presented a difficult problem. Slavery was early considered a curse, and endeavor was made to prohibit the importation of Africans, but against the royal veto nothing could be done. While the Revolution was yet in progress the General Assembly banned the traffic in negroes and repealed the colonial prohibition on manumission. To ameliorate the condition of the negro became the object of anti-slavery sentiment. During the last quarter of the eighteenth century abolition societies flourished, while from the dawn of the nineteenth colonization loomed constantly larger in the public mind. The tide of anti-slavery feeling was rising.

Abruptly all this was changed. By 1835 anti-slavery feeling had reached its greatest strength and was already receding. Its champions were few and hard pressed. Virginia had turned to the defence of slavery. In the following pages the author has endeavored to portray the events and circumstances which were productive of this change.

To Dr. John H. Latané of the Johns Hopkins University, under whose guidance and direction this study was carried on, the author wishes to express his appreciation and thanks. From the late Dr. Edward

Raymond Turner, also of the Johns Hopkins, he received counsel and assistance. Dr. Preston Slosson of the University of Michigan contributed helpful suggestions. Miss Elizabeth D. Dixon examined the entire manuscript with critical and sympathetic care. It is a pleasure to acknowledge the courtesy of Miss Elizabeth S. Iddings and Miss Katherine Dudley of the Johns Hopkins University Library, and of Dr. H. R. McIlwaine, Mr. M. P. Robinson, Miss Johnson, Miss Bass, and Mrs. Pollard of the Virginia State Library.

T. M. W.

CONTENTS

CHAPTER I

Virginia's Attitude Towards Slavery, 1619-1829

In the annals of American history 1619 occupies a peculiar and important place. To the student of government this year signifies the extension of the British representative system to America; for it was at this time that Governor Yeardley called into being the House of Burgesses, the prototype of legislative assemblies in the United States. To the chivalrous, given to the worship of the fair sex, 1619 recalls the arrival of a ship laden with ninety young women seeking husbands. In the same year occurred a third event of perhaps equal importance; in the language of John Rolfe, " about the last of August came in a Dutch man of warre that sold us twenty negars." [1]

Though purchasers were found for these negroes, further importation was slight for a quarter of a century. At the end of thirty years but three hundred were to be found in the colony, and that too despite the granting, in 1635, of head rights for negroes as well as white servants.

Though negroes were brought in increasing lots during the middle of the century, white indentured servants were the chief source of labor. By 1671

[1] The Government Surrendered to Sir George Yeardley, in *Captain John Smith's Works,* Edward Arber ed. (1884), p. 541.

1

Virginia counted six thousand indentured whites against two thousand negroes. During the next dozen years the number of the former doubled while the latter increased by a third. Evidently the colonist preferred white labor to black, even though the Royal African Company with the Duke of York at its head offered large shipments of negroes. Not to be thwarted by the obstinacy of the colony, the Duke dried up the source of white labor with legal enactments. After 1683 white indentured labor yielded place to slavery.[2]

In consequence of the increase of the black population the colony was obliged to give to the system of slavery legal status. Hitherto recognition had been accorded this property by way of regulatory acts, but title had been held, as upon cattle, by sale and possession. In 1670 an act was passed declaring that all " servants not being Christian imported into the colony by shipping " should be " slaves for their lives."[3] Twelve years later this was amended to include " all servants . . . . whether Negroes, Moors, Mollatoes, or Indians," provided that they were not from Christian countries or Christians themselves. In 1705 they were declared real estate, but the lapse of forty-three years found them classified as " chattels personal."[4]

---

[2] James C. Ballagh, *A History of Slavery in Virginia*, pp. 7-10.

[3] William W. Henning, *Statutes at Large: Being a Collection of All the Laws of Virginia*, etc., II, 283, 491.

[4] Ibid., V, 432.

To cope with the slave's propensity for crimes of all degrees, stringent laws were enacted. Slaves were forbidden to remain on other plantations longer than four hours unless bearing passes from their owners.[5] Slaves in hiding in woods or swamps were outlawed and left to the tender mercy of any who would capture or kill them if capture proved difficult. Excessive punishment " not touching life " was sanctioned and dismemberment allowed for certain crimes. Did more than five slaves meet to " consult, advise, or conspire, to rebel " or to commit murder they should " suffer death and be utterly excluded the benefit of clergy." [6] To discourage theft slaves were forbidden to own cattle and hogs. By no means were they to possess or use firearms.

In 1698 the Royal African Company lost exclusive control of the trade and sharp competition arose. As the number of negroes increased Virginia came to consider them a menace and sought to limit their importation. But the repugnance of the colonists was more than matched by the greed of British dealers. A slight tax upon negroes measured the power of the colonial assembly. Indeed, in 1724 a colonial act placing a duty on liquors and slaves became the subject of a report to the Privy Council sitting at Whitehall. Inasmuch as " This duty must have been a great hindrance to the negro Trade " the committee advised rejection of the act and cen-

[5] Ibid., III, 86, 458.
[6] Ibid., IV, 126.

sured the governor for permitting it to go into effect
before it had been approved. It was further advised
that he be ordered " not on any pretence whatsoever
[to] presume to Give his assent to any act of this
kind for the future " without inserting a suspending
clause.[7] This policy was continued down to the outbreak of the Revolution.

But slavers were not to enjoy royal favor forever.
With independence came opportunity for correcting
this state of affairs. Some there were who wished
to see the abolition of slavery undertaken at once,[8]
but in the maelstrom of revolution this step so
fraught with good was not taken. A large half-step
shut Virginia's gates to this trade:

> Be it enacted by the General Assembly, That . . . . no
> slave or slaves shall hereafter be imported into this Common-
> wealth by sea or land, nor shall any slave so imported be sold
> or bought by any person whatsoever.
> II. Every person hereafter importing slaves into this com-
> monwealth contrary to this act shall forfeit and pay the sum

[7] " MS. Report of a Committee of the Privy Council," *Colonial
Papers* 1721-35, Archives, Virginia State Library, Richmond, Va.

[8] Jefferson had prepared a draft for adoption with the new constitution freeing the slaves born after a date to be fixed by the State.
Upon attaining determined ages, by which time the masters should
have had time to recoup themselves for the cost of rearing, the slaves
would automatically become the property of the State to be transported beyond the limits of the United States.

St. George Tucker expounded to his classes at William and Mary
College the virtues of a similar system differing only in detail; freedom should be granted to females born after a given date, by them
to be transmitted to all their offspring. (*A Dissertation on Slavery
with a Proposal for the General Abolition of It in the State of
Virginia*, 1796.)

of one thousand pounds for every slave so imported and every person selling or buying any such slaves shall in like manner forfeit and pay the sum of five hundred pounds for every slave so sold or bought . . . .

III. And be it further enacted, That every slave imported into this commonwealth contrary to the true intent and meaning of this act shall upon such importation become free.[9]

Travelers with their personal attendants were exempted from this act. Citizens of other States removing to Virginia were permitted to bring in their slaves upon taking oath of their intention to abide by this act.[10]

Not content with closing the door upon slavery in accordance with this act, friends of the negro bound themselves together to form abolition societies. These early societies chiefly interested themselves in thwarting the efforts of kidnappers and in prompting manumissions. All too common during the close of this century was the practice of kidnapping free negroes and selling them south. For a while the societies flourished,[11] but in the nature of the case their work was self-destructive, for as the number

[9] Hening, IX, 471.

[10] The following oath was to be taken within ten days after arrival. "I, A. B., do swear that my removal to the State of Virginia was with no intention to evade the act for preventing the farther importation of slaves, nor have I brought with me . . . . any slaves with an intent of selling them nor have any . . . . been imported from Africa or any of the West India Islands since the first day of November, 1778. So help me God." (Ibid., IX, 472.)

[11] For a brief account of the abolition societies see Mary Stoughton Locke, *Anti-Slavery in America*.

of freed negroes increased, society became increasingly indisposed to tolerate a large class of negroes beyond the strict rule of slavery.

While numerically weak the free negro was despised and neglected, but growing into strength he caught the eye of the Assembly. By the end of the seventeenth century this body found it expedient to forbid manumission unaccompanied by provision for the removal of the negro within six months. Did any master grant his slave freedom without providing for his removal, he was liable to a fine of fifty pounds sterling wherewith the church wardens of the parish should remove the erstwhile slave.[12]

Acts of 1723 and 1748 reaffirmed this prohibition but permitted manumission for " meritorious services to be adjudged and allowed by the governor and council." [13] But with the change in government thirty years later these acts were superseded and the colonial prohibition was reversed. Masters were permitted to manumit their slaves by deed or will.[14] Kidnapping and selling free negroes was forbidden under pain of death.[15]

Encouraged by acts facilitating manumission, Virginia philanthropy increased by leaps and bounds. Fed by a swelling tide of emancipations and protected against those who would deprive them of their

[12] Hening, III, 87.
[13] Ibid., IV, 132; V, 112.
[14] Ibid., XI, 39.
[15] Ibid., XII, 182, 531.

liberty for pecuniary gain, the free black population soon attained alarming size. From less than 3,000 [16] at the close of the Revolution, they grew to 12,254 by 1790, and in 1800 numbered 19,981. Despite unfriendly legislation of 1806 again conditioning manumission upon removal, Virginia counted in 1810, 30,269; in 1820, 36,760, and in 1830, 46,729.[17] The last was more than one-seventh of the free colored population of the United States.

Despised by the whites and denied privileges that would have been his had his skin been lighter, limited in the capacity for earning an honest living yet denied access to the barns of the slaveholder, the free black was in many ways less fortunate than his brother in bondage. Scarcely owning the dust on the clothes he wore, he was almost of necessity driven to petty larceny to eke out an existence. In too many cases he exchanged perpetual slavery to a master for intermittent slavery to the State. Convicts were recruited in disproportionate numbers from among the freed negroes.

Quickly it was learned of experience that to emancipate was but half the task. While the negro was but little benefited, the peace and security of society, because of his almost sure recourse to crime, were to that extent further jeopardized. William Meade, later bishop of Virginia, writing in 1832,

[16] Beverly B. Munford, *Virginia's Attitude Toward Slavery and Secession*, p. 42.

[17] Jedediah Hotchkiss, *Virginia, A Geographical and Political Summary*, p. 266.

2

expressed the opinion that the negroes were little
benefited by emancipation alone:

I have thought, read, conversed, written, and spoken much
on this subject for the last fifteen years. I have travelled
through all the length and breadth of our land, and witnessed
the condition of all negroes, bond and free; conversed fully
with them, their owners, and their philanthropic friends; and
every year only rivets the conviction more deeply in my mind,
that to do them real good they must be separated from those
of a different color.[18]

A clergyman declared that " having formerly set
free a number of colored people who are now vaga-
bonds, I have done them no profit, but injured society. For this there is no remedy, as I have no
control over them. Those still in my possession, I
cannot conscientiously emancipate, unless they shall
be removed by the Society to Liberia." [19] The Sage
of Monticello warned against the danger to society.
To a distinguished foreign observer the danger was
equally patent:

I am obliged to confess that I do not regard the abolition
of slavery as a means of warding off the struggle of the two
races in the Southern States. The Negroes may long remain
slaves without complaining; but if they are once raised to the
level of freemen, they will soon revolt at being deprived of
almost all civil rights; and as they cannot become the equals
of the whites, they will speedily show themselves as ene-
mies. . . . . When I contemplate the condition of the South,
I can only discover two alternatives which may be adopted

[18] Early L. Fox, " The American Colonization Society " in *Johns
Hopkins Studies*, XXXVII, 346.
[19] Ibid., XXXVII, 344.

by the white inhabitants of those States; viz. either to emancipate the Negroes and to intermingle with them, or, remaining isolated from them, to keep them in slavery as long as possible. All intermediate measures seem to me likely to terminate, and that shortly, in the most horrible of civil wars, and perhaps in the extirpation of one or the other of the two races.[20]

Despite the heavy burden of manumission and removal, some there were who, convinced of the injustice of slavery and conscious of the awful responsibility attendant upon the possession of human beings, carried on the work of emancipation. If burdens were heavy, masters were generous. In not a few cases a large fraction of the estate was dedicated to the removal of newly made freemen. A brief extract from the will of John Smith of Sussex, probated March 1826, attests the sincerity of his desire and the pecuniary burden on his estate:

At the death of my beloved wife, I direct that all of my negroes without regard to age, sex, or condition, with all their future increase, be . . . . sent to the African Colonization Settlement . . . . I do hereby give and grant to each of the said negroes so emancipated . . . . one good serviceable hat, one pair shoes and stockings, blanket, and one year's provisions, exclusive of ship provisions on board, to carry with them . . . . [and] direct my executors to pay all expenses of removing said emancipated slaves out of any money that may be in their hands belonging to my estate.[21]

[20] De Tocqueville, *Democracy in America* (1898), I, 486.
[21] Munford, *Virginia's Attitude Toward Slavery and Secession*, p. 110.

The will of William H. Fitzhugh ensured the con-
tinuation of the work which he so sponsored during
his life:

After the year 1850 I leave all my negroes unconditionally
free, with the privilege of having the expenses of their removal
to whatever places of residence they may select, defrayed. And
as an encouragement to them to emigrate to the American
Colony on the coast of Africa, where I believe their happiness
will be most permanently secure, I desire not only that the
expense of their transportation may be paid but that the sum
of fifty dollars shall be paid to each one so emigrating on his
or her arrival in Africa.[22]

During the summer of 1800 Virginia was rudely
shocked by the disclosure of a widely concerted plan
of insurrection directed by Gabriel, a slave owned
by Thomas Prosser of Henrico County. Arms had
been gathered and the leaders spoke of some thousands of men to join at the first outbreak. While a
subaltern covertly fired the water front of Richmond, the main force led by Gabriel thought to seize
the magazine in the Capital Square. A torrential
rain on the appointed night caused the postponement
of the outbreak and afforded the government time
to frustrate the conspiracy, revealed a few hours
before the time of meeting.

Punishment followed rapidly. Gabriel and twenty
odd of his followers ended their days upon the gibbet,
while some ten others left the State in the watchful,
if not tender, care of the slave dealer. Anxious to

[22] Ibid., p. 113.

effect a more humane riddance of " suspects," the
Assembly, in secret, adopted a resolution author-
izing Governor Monroe to correspond with the President to the end of acquiring lands " without the
limits of this State, whither persons obnoxious to
the laws or dangerous to the peace of Society may
be removed.[23]

At the next session, while letters were yet passing
between Monroe and Jefferson, the legislature, out-
growing the contracted program of punishing offenders, caught the vision of a colony peopled by
such free blacks as should choose to emigrate or be
emancipated for the purpose, and directed Monroe
to consider the new project.[24]

In vain Jefferson sought to effect a union of the
blacks of Virginia with those of the British colony
of Sierra Leone.[25]

In the vastness of the newly acquired territory to
the west of the Mississippi the colonizationists vis-
ualized the dream of their hearts. There adequate
territory could be secured without the let or hindrance of any foreign power. Early in 1805 the Assembly renewed the attempt to secure the longed-
for land. This too was in vain. Though so many
times thwarted the House of Delegates had not yet

[23] Calendar Virginia State Papers, IX, 195. See also *Writings of
James Monroe*, Stanilaus M. Hamilton, ed. (1900), III, 292-295.

[24] *Writings of Monroe*, IX, 336-338.

[25] Sierra Leone was established by British philanthropists for slaves
that in one way or another had left their homes during the Revolution for Canada and England. Liberia was yet to be founded, 1820.

given up. In 1816 a resolution directing the governor to solicit the aid of the President in securing a strip of land along the Pacific coast was adopted by an eloquent majority, 137-9.[26] The Senate concurred with but little opposition.[27] Elsewhere events were taking place to give these dreams reality.

To the north, too, there were those who deplored the existence of the negro in their midst and sought to remove those that were free. Upon this high ground Henry Clay and Daniel Webster, Robert Finley of New Jersey and John Randolph of Roanoke, Jefferson and Marshall, Bushrod Washington, Francis Scott Key, Charles Mercer, and William Brodnax could meet, forget their private and political differences, and pool their energies. On December 16, 1816, a little company met in Washington to discuss the problem of colonizing the free blacks. From this meeting evolved the American Colonization Society.

From the first the Society found generous support in personnel and pecuniary backing along the banks of the James. To Virginia it turned for its third and fourth presidents, Madison and Clay. Auxiliary chapters sprang up in Norfolk, Fredericksburg, Petersburg, Alexandria, Lynchburg, Wheeling, Charleston, and Richmond, the last under the presidency of John Marshall. The year 1826 brought a

[26] Journal of the House of Delegates of the General Assembly of Virginia, 1816-17, p. 90. We shall refer to this below as *House Journal*.

[27] Journal of the Senate of the General Assembly of Virginia, 1816-17, p. 21.

legislative appropriation to aid in the work and two
years later the Colonization Society of Virginia was
established. Again Marshall was called to the chair.
The names of Tyler, Floyd, Charles Mercer, William Fitzhugh, and Bishop Meade were on its rolls.
In 1831 Virginia supported thirty-four societies
boasting seventy-three life members, at which time
the twelve states north of Delaware contained but
ninety-seven societies counting one hundred and
fourteen life members.[28]

During the first quarter of the nineteenth century Virginia was undergoing economic and social
changes soon to cause political friction between the
major sections of the State and ultimately to rend
it in vain. Economically, the lower counties continued along traditional lines. Slaves multiplied;
plantations stretched themselves over wide acres;
younger sons with their slaves joined the trek to the
southwest; and the weary soil pointed the poor and
industrious whites to the mountains.

In contrast, the rude and mountainous country beyond the Alleghanies supported a rapidly growing,
sturdy and industrious yeomanry,—farmers, arti-
sans, shopkeepers, and mechanics. The topography
of the country precluded the entrance of the plantation system. Cut off by mountains, lacking both
adequate land and water highways, the people of the
West early felt the need for canals. The environ-

[28] Alice D. Adams, *The Neglected Period of Anti-Slavery, 1808-31*,
p. 106.

ment was reflected in a bold spirit of self-reliance
and a sense of democratic equality. With this' political complexion and a keen desire for an extensive canal program, the West was sure to run
athwart the interests of the East.

The constitution of 1830 was the fruit of the long
struggle waged by Western Virginia that she might
exert an influence in the councils of the State in pro-
portion to her numerical importance. In the General
Assembly of 1828 the counties east of the Alleghanies, with a white population of 348,873, had one
hundred and thirty-four delegates and fifteen senators, while only eighty delegates and nine senators
represented the 254,196 whites to the West; [29] or
stated differently, 3,177 whites of the latter were
equated against 2,603 of the former in determining
representation in the House of Delegates. Comparison of single counties reveals more glaring injustice.
While Harrison had quadrupled, Randolph tripled,
Franklin and Rockingham doubled between 1790 and
1820, King William, Northumberland, and Prince
William had lost population. Warwick's 620 whites,
forty-seven less than she counted in 1790, enjoyed
equal representation with the 16,708 whites of
Shenandoah.[30]

To the attack upon the freehold basis of suffrage,
the East replied that this would be no hardship did

[29] Charles H. Ambler, *Sectionalism in Virginia*, p. 136.
[30] Hotchkiss, *A Political and Geographical Summary*, etc., pp. 261-
266. McGregor, *The Disruption of Virginia*, p. 28.

the people of the West have a real interest in the
State. Land there was so cheap that any man with
the will and industry could easily acquire freehold
property and the franchise. Indeed the real suffer-
ers were the mechanics, traders, merchants, preachers, lawyers, and leaseholders of the Tidewater and
Piedmont counties where land values closed this
avenue to political expression.

The slave-holding East opposed reform, fearing
increased taxation for internal improvements and in
its train the dissolution of their chief wealth. Did
not the East pay three-fourths of the total revenue,
one-third of which accrued from the levy on slaves,
while the West received more money from the
treasury than it put in? But though the latter's
financial capacity was slight, its hunger for canals
seemed insatiable. Were white manhood suffrage
made the rule, power would pass from the East to
a West practically without slaves. The real fear
of slaveholders, the fundamental cause of opposition, was voiced later by Upshur when he declared
that if control of the legislature passed to the West
with very little slave property, it would not fail to
saddle the burden of government upon that property
resident largely in the East. Justice demanded that
the power to tax rest in the hands of those to whom
the government looked for revenue.

Against the determined opposition of threatened
slavedom, reformers made way but slowly. They
were not to be deterred. Successive defeats only

exasperated them and their constituents. If nothing could be accomplished in Richmond, the citadel of conservatism, they would move the capital westward. In 1823 Baldwin moved in the House of Delegates that the capital be changed. His motion was rejected, but it woke the East to the temper of the West. The next year, the natal year of Thomas Jackson, the House of Delegates passed a convention bill, but the Senate was obdurate. This last stronghold was finally carried on January 31, 1828. The people were to express their wish to revise or preserve the current constitution.

To the question " Shall there be a Convention to amend the Constitution of the Conmmonwealth?" the voters answered " Yes " twenty thousand strong.[31] The sectional nature of the conflict was strikingly reflected in the vote. Below the fall line, the Eastern Shore excepted, the poll was solidly against the convention, while with minor exceptions the rest of the State voted in the affirmative. Despite later rather neutral service, the valley districts joined the transmontane country to call the convention.

The ensuing House of Delegates reflected with peculiar accuracy the political wishes of the State. Well might its members feel that they came with a special mandate from their constituents, for many

---

[31] The vote announced by the Executive was 20,825 for, and 16,595 against; subsequent returns from Harrison County increased the affirmative vote. (*Constitutional Whig*, Sept. 3, 1828.)

had gained or retained their seats because of their attitude towards a constitutional convention. Small wonder then that the convention proved to be the engulfing problem from the very first. Convened December 1, the Assembly was called at once to the main issue and five days later Nelson was appointed chairman of a committee to consider so much of the Governor's Message as related to that subject. On the twentieth Nelson reported a bill to call a convention.

Public interest was keen. The press carried *in extenso* the debates in the Legislature while the countryside responded with '' Hints to Friends of Convention,'' local meetings, resolutions, and memorials. '' An Earnest Appeal '' clamored for a white basis for the convention. Any other would be worse than none; it would but renew evils '' which if we have the manhood to attempt it, we can now shake off forever.'' [32] '' A Clodhopper,'' equally bombastic, wrote to set the western delegates straight about the whole matter. The East had agreed to the convention in order to satisfy the West and to effect a few minor reforms. There was not the least idea of giving the West control. Not unless the people of the East were worse than fools, would any basis but that of population and taxation combined be adopted. Let the West be grateful that she was permitted to meet in convention at all. Some wrote to extol the large blessings of current institutions, but their effu-

[32] *Richmond Enquirer,* January 10, 1829.

sions were well nigh lost in the flood of reform liter-
ature. The atmosphere was heavily charged and
danger hung on every cloud. The editor of the *Enquirer* warned against hasty or violent action.

Debate turned chiefly upon three plans proposed
as proper bases for the equitable representation of
the several sections of the State. The first plan proposed to make the convention but the image of the
House of Delegates with all its imperfections. Regardless of size or wealth, each county should send
the same number of delegates. The second, or congressional district plan, would make use of the elec-
toral divisions into which the State was divided for
the election of representatives to Congress. As the
slave population was reflected in this division in
accordance with the three-fifths principle,[33] eastern
gentlemen warmly espoused the second plan and
western as stoutly opposed it. The East was un-
faithful to its first love, the equal county plan, because of the impossibility of forcing it upon the
West.

The third, senatorial district, would fashion the
convention after the Virginia Senate. Let the
twenty-four districts have equal delegations. On
the one hand, this plan would yield the West greater
power because of the more equitable distribution of
seats in the Senate; on the other, the East would re-

---

[33] To the number of whites was added three-fifths of the slaves.
Thus the East, having a large slave population, would have undue
power as the West looked at it.

ceive a modicum of power in excess of its *pro rata* strength in consequence of changes in population since the distribution of senatorial seats in 1810. The extreme Western basis was that of white manhood suffrage.

Philip Doddridge, the champion of white manhood suffrage, attacked the original bill based upon congressional districts. One could claim representation for slaves on but one of two grounds: either that they were men or that they were property. Did Tidewater politicians declare them men, Doddridge would refer them to the war claims against Great Britain for property stolen or destroyed during the Revolution. Even the Federal Constitution could see but three-fourths of a man in a slave. Were they declared entitled to representation because they were property, he would view cattle with new respect. Were not they property also? Was property *per se* to be clothed with political power? Whatever the form of property the idea was ridiculous. The West could never agree to equate white men against slaves.

Newton conceded that they were property and fell back on the argument that " representation ought to be based upon both persons and property; that taxation and representation ought to bear some just relation to each other."[34]

Feeling was too intense to admit of rapid progress, but happily about the middle of January Terrill

[34] *Richmond Enquirer,* January 8, 1829.

proposed a middle ground, an arbitrary assignment of representation. Let the counties be graduated according to population and given the representation determined for their respective grades. To this plan, amended slightly by Gordon, a majority of the House rallied, 123 to 81.[35]

In the Senate debate followed the already well worn lines. Morgan's amendment thrust manhood suffrage into the limelight, but it was too radical to survive the onslaught of slavedom. The strongest rival of the Terrill plan embodied in the bill as reported to the Senate, was the Fitzhugh senatorial district plan. Early in the discussion it was proposed to fix the delegations at five, for this number seemed most suitable to create a body at once large enough to represent all the interests of the State, yet small enough for the expeditious handling of business. Akin to this plan was Allen's proposal to adopt senatorial districts with a minimum delegation of three with possible accession of one, two, or three as the population of each justified.

George Dromgoole delivered a strong speech in defence of the Eastern position on slavery representation. All were agreed that property must be secure. Only by infusing its influence into the very organs of government, Dromgoole avowed, could property be secured. In what more expeditious manner could this be accomplished than by allotting representation according to the compound ratio of

[35] *House Journal*, 1828-29, p. 148.

people and property? Were it proposed to distribute political power among individuals according to their possessions, one might fear the evils of oligarchy. The compound ratio would guarantee property without creating a small ruling class. Individually the vote of one man would avail as much as that of another, while the increment of representation given the county by way of securing masters in the possession of their slaves would bear an intimate relation to the magnitude of that form of property. The abhorrence of the idea of allowing representation for negroes shown by gentlemen from the West Dromgoole thought insincere and declared as his belief that if " the relative number of colored persons in the two sections of the State were reversed, ... the proposition [slave representation] would then lose more than half its frightful deformities." [36]

In answer to the demand that taxation should be linked with representation, as the only means of securing property, Wilson naïvely argued that slave owners had little cause to be alarmed; owners of few slaves because they had little property to be taxed, and owners of many because they would receive compensation in police protection.

February 9 witnessed the culmination of the struggle in the triumph of the senatorial plan. A compromise, drawn by Taylor, giving to the West senatorial districts, and to the East equal representation and the current franchise, mustered to its sup-

[36] *Richmond Enquirer*, April 7, 1829.

port a majority of the Senate. The first section ordered the qualified voters to assemble in May next and elect in each senatorial district " four discreet and proper persons as members of said convention."

The following day the clerk of the House of Delegates summed up the action of the Senate in the brief record: " The Senate have passed the bill entitled ' An Act to Organize a Convention ' with an amendment." The " amendment " completely changed the House bill, substituting senatorial districts for Terrill's counties. Notwithstanding the heated debate that attended the production of the original bill, the House adopted the Senate bill, 114 to 93.[37]

[37] *House Journal,* 1828-29, pp. 178, 184.

CHAPTER II

The Constitutional Convention of 1829-30

The constitutional convention of 1829-30 proved a good thing for the hostelries and boarding houses of Richmond. Stages entering the city carried heavy loads and taverns along the way enjoyed unwonted patronage. The novelty of the meeting and the questions at issue sufficed to make the convention the chief object of interest and topic of discussion at fireside and husting. Beside the interest normally attending a meeting such as this, the high talent it counted made Richmond the Mecca of both the curious and serious-minded of counties far and near and attracted distinguished visitors from other States.

In truth the Convention could claim to command the ability of the State in unique completeness. There in the glorious twilight of prominent life were the venerated Madison, Monroe, and Marshall. There John Randolph, orator *par excellence,* moved amid the uneasy watchfulness of opponents and friends. Master of bitter irony, he was feared by all. Where his bony finger next would follow a cutting thrust none could tell, but all might fear. There with the mantle of victory about his tortured frame Governor William Giles capped a long life of devoted service to his native State. Mighty partisan had he been, but now disease obliged him to hold his blow until a younger parliamentary strategist should call. To Benjamin Watkins Leigh fell the mantle of leadership.

Leigh was excellently prepared for the part. Native ability schooled by wide reading and sharpened by forensic battle before the local bar, earned him the reputation of a profound lawyer unsurpassed by any in the State. Selected to compile the Code of 1819, he was better acquainted with the course of legislation than any of those about him. A quick mind ever alert, foreseeing objections and their counter thrust, made him a dangerous foe and a skillful leader.

The western cohorts also were lead by a member of the Richmond bar, Chapman Johnson, a lawyer recognized throughout the State as an ornament to the court before which he practised. Gifted with a commanding presence, rivaling the famous Randolph in forensic flourish, and possessed of great intellectual powers, he was the best who could be brought against Leigh. A tendency to abstract, obtuse argument carried to too great length was his greatest weakness. Seconding Johnson, Philip Doddridge, in bombastic and impulsive outbursts, kept the East ever mindful of the extreme Western will to achieve manhood suffrage, within the State if possible, without if necessary.

Judge Upshur, Philip Barbour, Charles Mercer and William H. Fitzhugh deserve mention. Somewhat overshadowed, there was a group of younger men soon to bear the brunt of leadership in a more fateful crisis. We refer to William H. Brodnax, Samuel McDowell Moore, and William O. Goode. From them we shall hear in the slavery debate of 1831-32.

During the summer there emerged from Augusta County a petition to the Convention which perhaps increased the unrest among the lower counties. After a flattering salutation it called upon the Convention to consider the slavery of the negro and the feasibility of a constitutional provision for a system of emancipation.

Waiving consideration of religion and humanity, slavery was denounced upon the ground of political wisdom and public safety. The experience of the petitioners confirmed the doctrine of economists that slave labor is '' vastly less '' productive than that of freemen. Upon the land it was productive of the most deleterious consequences, exceeded only by its effects upon the moral fibre of the youth '' growing up with a contempt of steady industry as a low servile thing, which contempt induces idleness and all its attendant effeminacy, vice, and worthlessness.'' The future could offer nothing better, but in its stead worse degradation, were slavery allowed to continue gnawing away the very vitals of the body politic. Every year witnessed the further growth of the horrid parasite. Were the black flood not damned, and that at an early date, the State would be overwhelmed with the direst ruin.

In view of these considerations, the petitioners could not but consider slavery " an evil greater than the aggregate of all others that beset " them and pray its removal. In the execution of such a program they pledged their support.[1]

Just after mid-day Monday, October 5, the attention of delegate and spectator centered upon a small aged gentleman. In a voice scarcely audible a few feet away he called attention to James Monroe as the person most suitable to preside. There was no opposition. James Madison conducted his venerated nominee to the chair.

Accepting the honor, Monroe pledged his best abilities to the cause that called the body into being. He frankly admitted that experience had shown defects in the constitution. Wisdom demanded their removal and he for one would not oppose. Let every man face the fact squarely and acquit himself to the best of his abilities. With this candor and spirit, Monroe declared that their labors would justify the hopes with which they had been dispatched to Richmond.

Organization consumed several days. George W. Munford was elected clerk. Four committees were appointed to consider the major parts of the constitution; of these we need consider only the committee on the legislative department and that for the " Bill of Rights and other matters not referred to

[1] *Daily Richmond Whig,* July 14, 1829, reprint from *Staunton Spectator.*

the foregoing committee.''[2] Leigh was appointed chairman of the first.

Leigh found the committee on the legislative department difficult to control. There sat the triumvirs of the West, Johnson, Doddridge, and Cooke. Upon Madison, eager for a workable compromise, he could not implicitly rely. The West pushed its measures vigorously and despite all the chairman could do the committee was on the whole favorable to reform.

At the first meeting Philip Doddridge offered two resolutions to the effect that representation in both houses of the Assembly should be based on white population. Despite the renewed use of the property argument handed down by the late Assembly, the West was able to muster a majority for the resolution touching the House of Delegates. The second, concerning the Senate, was lost because of a tie effected by the shift of one vote. Upon the first measure Madison voted with the West, but on the second he took the opposite side. The best explanation seems that he was seeking a compromise. Not content with this single triumph, Doddridge subse-

[2] The Legislative Committee was composed of B. W. Leigh, Brodnax, Tyler, Anderson, Johnson, Beirne, Mason, Randolph, Madison, Mercer, Cooke, Pendleton, George, Roane, Chapman, Summers, Doddridge, Green, Tazewell, Campbell of Bedford, Townes, Pleasants, Taliaferro, and Joynes.

The other of: Samuel Taylor, Goode, Clopton, Williamson, Moore, Baxter, Urquhart, Logan, Opie, Donaldson, Byars, William P. Taylor, Oglesby, See, Wilson, Macrae, Prentis, Saunders, Stuart, Massie, and Read. (*Proceedings and Debates of the Virginia State Convention of 1829-30*, pp. 22, 23.)

quently moved the adoption of a suffrage amendment in substantially the form reported by the committee. In this too he was successful.

On October 23 the Bill of Rights committee declared that " Equal numbers of qualified voters are entitled to equal representation throughout the State." On the morrow Madison read the report of the Legislative Committee. The first resolution read: " Resolved, That in the apportionment of representation in the House of Delegates regard should be had to the white population exclusively." [3] Acquainted with the rigidity of the old system, the second resolution ordered that a census be taken in 1831, 1845, and at least every twenty years thereafter.

The third resolution extended the suffrage almost to the extreme—white manhood suffrage—demanded by the West. To the old freeholders with minimum assessment were added those who were for six months possessed of freehold property, whether assessed or not. Holders of vested estates in remainder or reversion were next admitted. Those leasing land for five years, at least one unexpired, were enfranchised and finally he " who for twelve months next preceding has been a housekeeper and head of a family . . . . and who shall have been assessed with a part of the revenue of the Commonwealth within the preceding year and actually paid the same," was permitted to enter the charmed

[3] *Proceedings and Debates*, p. 39.

circle. Men born beyond the confines of Virginia were allowed the vote upon completing five years residence, the last two in the place of voting.

Slaveholders were not long in answering this assault. On the twenty-sixth Judge Green moved to amend the first resolution by the substitution of " and taxation combined " for " exclusively.'' Debate was postponed until the auditor should have prepared tax and population lists showing the relative condition of the four sections of the State, Tidewater, Piedmont, Valley, and Transmontane.

To Leigh's challenge to show reason for the adoption of the report " which in effect proposes to put the power of controlling the wealth of the State into hands different from those which hold that wealth, a plan which declares that representation shall be regulated by one ratio and contribution by another,"[4] Cooke delivered an argument lacking that cardinal virtue, brevity. The report was itself a picture of logic and justice. Only in the people could one find the real source of political power. Did any doubt, let him but turn to the Declaration of Rights and find it implicitly declared that power is vested in and derived from the people. The second great principle of both the report and the Declaration is that all men are " equally free.'' None denied that the mechanic of Charleston, and the planter of Halifax were equally liable for military service. Both alike held claims for protection against the

[4] Ibid., p. 53.

State. The courts were open to both. Equally industrious, intelligent, and honest, they deserved
equal opportunity and consideration in political
affairs.

If these two principles were granted, but one conclusion was possible, that the rule of the majority
was the only proper and just one. Again Cooke invoked the Bill of Rights to confirm his reasoning.

Fear that inhabited the breast of eastern gentlemen and made them ready to see in their fellow-
citizens to the west a band of culprits anxious to
rob them of their property, albeit by legal means,
Cooke thought unreasoning and founded upon a false
conception of human nature. Men were not essentially corrupt and devoid of high motives. But if
these failed, self-interests still remained. For forty
years the East had held the power of taxation un-
disputed, yet not a single complaint was heard
along the Shenandoah or Kanawha. Only under the
scourge of war had herds grazing these fertile val-
leys been taxed and with the return of peace the tax
gatherer turned his face towards the lowlands.
Justice and self-interest combined to guide the hand
of the East. The speaker could boast of a constitu-
ency equally high in moral tone and keen in de-
tecting its real interest.

By a loose juggling of the auditor's figures, Cooke
discovered a slaveholding population of 409,000 out
of the 680,000 whites in Virginia. With a majority

of 138,000 [5] devoted to slavery, even the most timid needed no longer hesitate to support the proposed extension of the suffrage.

Were the mountaineer as morally strong and ill-disposed to rob his fellow citizen as Cooke claimed, Green called attention to a very concrete basis for fear, canals. Improvements of the James River recently voted solely for the benefit of the people beyond the Ridge found enthusiastic support among the delegates from that district. Just a short while before a scheme to expend $3,700,000 on a similar work received the vote of every western man. Only the year before another bill for a million dollars was supported by the same gentlemen.

He could have raised no objection had these gentlemen, so generous in laying out the funds of the State, been representatives of people equally generous in providing funds. As we have already seen the East contributed three-fourths of the revenue. Land below the Blue Ridge was taxed two and a half times as heavily as that beyond the Alleghanies. One-quarter of the revenue was realized from the tax on slaves east of the Ridge. If the West had the power, canals furnished a constant excitant and the slave tax the means of raising funds without sharing the burden.

Should the white basis be adopted great unrest would develop in the lower counties. Fearful for the safety of their property, '' jealousies and intermi-

nable hostility will be generated '' among these good
people against those they fear. Though the West
might feel angry and chagrined at the loss of political importance, were the compound basis adopted,
this would all pass away, for they '' can never feel
themselves insecure as to their property; for no
law can be passed in the Legislature affecting property at all, that will not be felt to a much greater
extent on this side of the mountains.'' [6]

Judge Upshur discovered another kind of majority. The gentleman from Frederick, Cooke, disclosed the features of majority-in-number, now he,
Upshur, unveiled the face of the forgotten sister,
'' majority-in-interest.'' He challenged anyone to
show that his protégée was not the real donor of
power. If one thought to find authorization for the
majority-in-number in social compacts, he must con-
fine his search to the Virginia constitution. But to
correct the faults of that instrument of government
was the sole *raison d'être* the Convention could plead.

Turning to nature, its supporters are equally unsuccessful in the search for a mandate to the majority-in-number to rule. On the contrary, they find
the endorsement of nature put upon the rule of
physical force. Let the mind but wander to a tribe
ruled by the majority thereof, women, children, and
the aged. Did any imagine the rule of this majority
would succeed in bringing else than ruin upon the
tribe? Could any imagine animals of the woods

[6] Ibid., p. 64.

swayed by consideration for the majority in anything other than power, albeit a minority in number?

The reason for the prevailing concept of majority
rule Upshur disclosed. This rule was founded upon
belief in the identity of majority in number and
majority in interest, upon the presumption that
the greater number possessed the greater interest.
When in the course of society the reason for it fails,
the rule no longer applies. " If the interests of the
several parts of the Commonwealth were identical,
it would be safe . . . . and proper that a majority
of persons " [7] should be the sole determinant in the
distribution of power. Both of the constituent ele-
ments of society, persons and property, must be incorporated in the instrument of government. Persons are protected against the machinations of foes
within and without. Property, in consequence of
taxes, is entitled to protection against fraud and
seizure. None are so interested in this protection as
the owner. In the compound basis every requirement
of good government is met.

The policy advocated by eastern gentlemen, Doddridge thought most vicious, one calculated to fasten
political slavery upon the West in the measure that
undue political importance was allowed for the protection of property. This might possibly be granted
for the present, but in the future this principle would
be intolerable. It was nowhere denied that while the

[7] Ibid., p. 70.

East would retain the preponderating portion of
the slave population, the white in the West would be
constantly increasing. Its hold upon the Assembly
continually diminishing, the East would demand increasing power. Every increase of the white population to the west of the Alleghanies would necessitate
a corresponding diminution of individual importance there that the relative strength of the two
sections might remain fixed.

Morris reiterated the statement that the end of
good government was two-fold, protection of property and persons. It was not enough to show that
all other than the white basis would limit political
and personal rights. It must also be shown that
property would not be placed in jeopardy. He sin-
cerely hoped that an instrument meeting both re-
quirements could be arranged, but sooner than
sacrifice either of these principles he would agree to
the adoption of two constitutions and the division
of the State.

In lurid terms he warned against the danger of
giving the West control. Were the slave tax raised
much higher, '' one of two things must happen, either
the master run away from the slave or the slave
from the master. . . . . Let it be known that this
separation of the master and his slave is not a voluntary thing on either side, but a matter of compulsion
[produced] by the . . . . passage of a law of emancipation or a tax law depriving the master of his
power of holding his slave and soon a sword will be

unsheathed that will be red with the best blood of this country before it finds its scabbard."[8]

On the thirty-first John Scott offered a short-lived resolution looking to a compromise. To Green's amendment he would add a clause basing the Senate wholly on the white population.[9]

In advocacy of the compound basis for the House, Scott called to mind a consequence likely to follow the repudiation of negro representation. Once Virginia made the white population the rule for the distribution of representation in her own councils, he thought it highly probable that she would be faced by a movement to limit her representation in Congress by the same measure. Of her twenty-two representatives, seven[10] were allotted for the slave population. Were gentlemen prepared to reduce their native State by casting away these seven votes? As surely as they adopted the white basis they strengthened the arm that would seize these votes and those of the other slave States at the first opportunity.

Monroe made a statement in explanation of his action when the vote should be taken upon Green's amendment. He would readily embrace manhood suffrage. The claims of the East and the West were alike reasonable, but, working on the adage that the best possible government is the best practical government, he should vote for the compound basis.

[8] *Proceedings and Debates,* p. 116.
[9] Ibid., p. 124.
[10] Ibid., p. 126.

However much one deplored it, the grip of slavery was too severe to admit of any hope of state emancipation. Only with Federal aid could its manacles be broken and its black victims freed. Any measure that fell short of their removal he would oppose vigorously. As this was beyond the means of Virginia he would vote to afford the Atlantic counties the security they demanded.

Leigh returned to the conflict with a carefully prepared statement of the taxes paid by the several sections of the State. Upon the Tidewater counties the land tax amounted to 31 cents per capita. The twenty-nine counties below the Blue Ridge were assessed 34 cents. The Valley paid 28 cents, while the land beyond yielded only 12 cents. The slave taxes for the same districts were respectively 24, 28, 7 and 3 cents. Grouped on either side of the Ridge, the lower paid an average land and slave tax of 32.7 and 26.8 cents, while the upper contributed but 19.6 and 5 cents.[11]

John Randolph was the focus of special interest. Weeks passed while his admirers waited in vain for his acrid contribution to the debate. Witnessed by only a few, there arose, upon the conclusion of Stanard's brilliant speech, a tall, ghost-like figure and the words "Mr. Chairman" fell from the lips of John Randolph, almost by magic filling the erstwhile quiet Capital Square with running visitors mysteriously aware that he was speaking. At once the hall and doorway were filled as the

[11] Ibid., p. 152.

gentleman from Charlotte in "bitter sarcasms, gratuitous imputations, and learned jests" defended the existing constitution and deprecated the "spirit of innovation."[12]

When Randolph took his seat the committee received the question on Green's amendment. The amendment was lost, 47-49.[13]

The next day, November 16, Leigh offered an amendment to the first resolution. Let the counties be apportioned representation in the House of Delegates with respect to the sum of their white and three-fifths of their slave population.[14]

The atmosphere was such as to hinder the expeditious dispatch of business. Debate upon representation seemed interminable. Feeling was intense. The committee wisely turned to the less volatile resolutions of the legislative report. Debate on the reports of the Judiciary and Executive Committees afforded further opportunity for passions to cool.

The third resolution of the legislative report extended the suffrage. There was little new light to be thrown upon this subject. Already nature and history had been exhausted in support of "majority in number." Weary of historical speculations, gentlemen were not disposed to tolerate their repetition, though Morpheus still offered relief. Constitutions of other States were reviewed to show the way

[12] Ibid., pp. 313, 336.
[13] Ibid., p. 321.
[14] Ibid., p. 322.

to a wider electorate. It must be admitted that the
East was less determined and united upon this matter than upon representation, but withal there was
enough in it to challenge the slaveholding aristoc-
racy, especially as it was proposed to distribute
representation according to the voting population.
Less directly, a non-property-holding electorate
threatened property of all description.

The fourth resolution of the report, continuing the
Senate in its same size, was made the peg on which
to hang another debate. That the white basis had
been adopted as the rule for the House of Delegates,
made it imperative for the East to secure a larger
senate incorporating the influence of property. Did
not inspection of the constitutions of other States
prove that the senate should be a third as large as
the lower house? The smallest House of Delegates
suggested was of one hundred and twenty members.
Let the senate be increased, apportioned according
to the Federal ratio, and given power to initiate
legislation. Here, the West argued, were all the
protection that could be needed, here upon a
" negro senate " and a white house the factions
could compromise.

Charles Mercer, white-basis partisan, offered his
panacea for the nervousness among the lower counties. Let there be incorporated in the new constitution a section linking horses, slaves, and land together for the purpose of taxation. Prohibit the
legislature from taxing any differently from the
other two. The West, having horses and lands, would

be thereby deterred from levying a confiscatory tax upon the " peculiar property " of the East.[15]

The action of the Convention in suspending debate upon the first resolution of the Legislative Report was not without result. On the twenty-fifth, Gordon offered an arbitrary schedule of representation based upon the average of the white, combined (persons and property), and Federal ratios. In a house of delegates of 120 and a senate of 30 he assigned representation as below:

Alleghany (1st District)....	26	Delegates,	7 Senators
Valley (2nd District)......	22		6
Piedmont (3rd District)....	38		9
Tidewater (4th District)...	34		8
	120		30

The second resolution in his plan provided for the future distribution of seats upon the average of the three ratios.[16] Benjamin Leigh suggested a similar plan for a house of 126, giving the districts 26, 23, 42, and 35 seats respectively.[17] John Marshall sponsored the Federal ratio, which he declared gave approximately the same power to the districts and offered the best basis for future action. According to his draft the districts would have 24, 23, 43, and 36 delegates.[18]

In his speech of acceptance James Monroe voiced his fear that the infirmities of age and disease would

[15] *Journal of the Convention*, 1829-30, p. 59.
[16] Ibid., p. 61.
[17] Ibid., p. 62.
[18] *Proceedings and Debates*, p. 499.

4

bind him in the discharge of the duties of his office. Reinforced by inclement weather, these dread foes left their mark. On December 8 Stanard was requested to occupy the chair and on the following day Philip Barbour of Orange was elected president pro tempore.

The selection of Philip Pendleton Barbour was indeed happy. Unlike his predecessor he brought from the Speaker's chair in the House of Representatives tact and a thorough knowledge of parliamentary law. Under his touch the most delicate point of order was established. Few could match his severe analysis of the question at hand and the logic of the proposed remedy. Eloquence, however polished, afforded no protection against the thrust of carefully prepared arguments. The master passion of his life was the law. Her handmaids, history and politics, he admired for their servitude. A short term on the bench of the District Court was followed by the crowning glory of his life, a seat in the Supreme Court. In his death his country, Judge Story declared, lost " not only a bright ornament but a pure and spotless patriot." [19]

On the twelfth the Convention received Monroe's resignation. Barbour was installed permanently in the President's chair.

Supplemented by an amendment offered by Upshur providing for future distribution of power,

[19] Hugh Blair Grigsby, *The Virginia Convention of 1829-30*, p. 37. Grigsby gives excellent short portraits of the more important characters in the Convention.

Gordon's plan was adopted. As reported to the Convention, December 15, it read:

Resolved, That the representation in the Senate and House of Delegates of Virginia, shall be apportioned as follows:

There shall be 13 Senators west of the Blue Ridge mountains, and 19 east of those mountains.

There shall be in the House of Delegates 127 members of whom 29 shall be elected from the district west of the Alleghany mountains; 24 from the Valley between the Alleghany and Blue Ridge; 40 from the Blue Ridge to the head of Tidewater, and 34 thence below.

Resolved, That the Legislature shall rearrange the representation in both Houses of the General Assembly once in every —— years upon a fair average of the following ratios, to wit: 1st, white population: 2, Federal Ratio; Provided that the number of the House of Delegates shall not exceed ——, nor the number of the Senate ——.[20]

At the same time the Committee virtually endorsed the suffrage resolution in the Report.

Debate in Convention upon Gordon's plan was brief. Four days sufficed for its adoption following the removal of the redistribution feature. The vote, 55-41,[21] was acutely sectional. With the majority were found but two delegates from the Valley and not one from the First District.

Despite the adoption of Gordon's plan the Convention was still overwhelmed by the question of representation. Again the white basis, offered by way of amendment, was defeated. Doddridge, Madi-

---

[20] *Convention Journal,* p. 78.

[21] Ibid., p. 126. It is here called Upshur's resolution, but pp. 78, 108-126 and the *Proceedings and Debates* plainly show it to be Gordon's.

son, Marshall, Johnson, B. W. Leigh, Tazewell, and Cooke, were appointed a committee "to report either a new constitution or amendments to the existing one."[22] Trying to frame a new constitution, gentlemen gained new respect for the old. Even Doddridge was less rabid.

By the second of January considerable progress had been made. Madison presented a new constitution. The third and fourth articles incorporated Gordon's plan and assigned seats to the several counties and districts as they were to be represented in the Assembly. Doubtless weary of futile debate and convinced of the advantage of handling the revision of the draft in a small committee, the Committee of the Whole contented itself with sundry minor amendments and allowed the smaller group a measure of discretion in revision. The House was increased first to 132 and finally to 134 members. The districts received 31, 25, 42 and 36 seats respectively.

At the last moment Judge Green rushed in an amendment to the ninth article to the effect that Virginia's whole representation in the national House of Representatives should be apportioned among the counties according to the Federal ratio.[23]

At eleven o'clock, January 14, the Convention was called to order in the First Baptist Church. The engrossing committee not ready to report, a recess was granted until two. At the appointed hour the Convention again assembled, but was for the same

22 Ibid., pp. 194, 195.
23 Ibid., p. 283.

reason adjourned until seven. The draft was then taken up promptly and with surprising dispatch adopted, 55-40.[24] With the exception of scarcely a half dozen changes the majority on this question was identically the one adopting Gordon's resolution. The half dozen changes rendered sectional lines even more acute, for the Valley on the present question cast but one vote in the affirmative. The gentlemen who voted in the affirmative were:

Barbour (President)
Jones
Leigh of Chesterfield
Taylor of Chesterfield
Giles
Brodnax
Dromgoole
Alexander
Goode
Marshall of Richmond
Tyler
Nicholas
Clopton
Mason of Southampton
Trezvant
Claiborne
Urquhart
Randolph
Leigh of Halifax
Logan
Venable
Madison
Holladay
Henderson
Cooke [Frederick County in the Valley]
Roane
Taylor of Caroline
Morris
Garnett
Barbour of Culpeper
Scott
Green
Marshall of Fauquier
Tazewell
Loyall
Prentis
Grigsby
Campbell of Bedford
Branch
Townes
Cabell
Martin
Stuart
Pleasants
Gordon
Thompson
Massie
Bates
Neale
Rose
Coalter
Joynes
Bayly
Upshur
Perrin

[24] *Proceedings and Debates,* p. 882.

The gentlemen voting against the adoption of the constitution were:

Anderson	Fitzhugh	Cloyd
Coffman	Osborne	Chapman
Harrison	Powell	Mathews
Williamson	Griggs	Oglesby
Baldwin	Mason of Frederick	Duncan
Johnson	Naylor	Laidley
M'Coy	Donaldson	Summers
Moore	Boyd	See
Beirne	Pendleton	Morgan
Smith	George	Campbell of Brooke
Miller	M'Millan	Wilson
Baxter	Campbell of Washington	Claytor
Stanard	Byars	Saunders
Mercer		

The next day the Constitution was endorsed by the President and committed to the Governor. On the motion of Benjamin Watkins Leigh the Convention adjourned sine die.

By and large the new constitution was a fair compromise. The suffrage had been widely extended on the one hand, while on the other representation still savoured of slavery. The representation of the Transmontane district was improved, while that of the Valley left little to be desired short of the white basis. The West failed to gain all it wished but there had been substantial concession at the expense of the East. If any had cause to reject the new constitution it was the lowland counties, for some of these were to have their representation reduced or merged. Plantation owners found themselves reduced to the level of the humblest householder of permanent residence. While few were completely satisfied, many, aware that "victory may be purchased too dearly," supported it as a satisfactory *modus vivendi* rather than live in "a state of feud, sectional animosity, and constant apprehension under one more theoretically excellent."[25]

Upon receiving a copy of the new constitution the Assembly busied itself with a bill to submit it to the people. It was determined "to submit the amended Constitution to the voters qualified thereby to vote for members of the General Assembly."[26] One might well have argued that the newly enfranchised voters would vote solidly for its adoption. In the East this may have been the fact, but the large majorities against it beyond the mountains too plainly showed the keen disappointment that white suffrage was denied.

During April and May the people gathered at their respective polls and cast 26,055 votes for and 15,563 against the new constitution.[27] The favorable votes were largely polled east of the Blue Ridge. West of the Alleghanies it was overwhelmingly rejected. Brooke with a clean slate of 371 unfavorable, more than offset Madison County with 256 favorable votes. Harrison polled the largest adverse majority, 8 for and 1112 against. Ohio, 3–643, and Logan, 2–255,

[25] *Daily Richmond Whig*, March 6, 1830.
[26] *Acts of The General Assembly*, 1829-30, p. 12.
[27] *House Journal*, 1830-31, Appendix, Document 1.

spoke eloquently their aversion. Warwick, loosing both of her delegates, mustered 63 votes against the constitution. The number voting must have been a disappointment, for despite the enlarged electorate the total vote barely exceeded forty thousand, less than five thousand more than the vote in 1828.

CHAPTER III

The High Tide of Anti-Slavery Feeling in Virginia

Anti-slavery feeling in Virginia reached its high tide in 1830. Relations between master and slave were during the years 1825-30 perhaps better than at any period since the birth of the nation. Manumissions were increasing and the lot of those retained in bondage was constantly improved by benevolent treatment. Severities of the law were ameliorated by personal kindness or entirely overlooked. That the lot of the slave was good is attested by the small number of runaways. Despite a slave population of 469,000, between May 1 and October 31, 1830, there appeared in three of the largest papers [1] but thirty-eight offers for, or notices of the incarceration of, runaways, barely double the number of rewards offered for horses lost, strayed, or stolen. The list of slaves executed or transported for major crimes is likewise surprisingly short. For the eleven years, 1820-30, we find only 265 or 24.09 annually,— less than .0061 per cent, convicted when the law allowed capital punishment more extensively than

[1] *Richmond Whig, Richmond Enquirer, Richmond Commercial Compiler,* May 19-21 of the last missing.

47

now.[2] Rape, arson, insurrection, robbery, murder, and conspiring " the murder of any ' free white ' " [3] were followed by execution, or, if the Governor showed mercy, transportation beyond the limits of the United States.

With the close of the second decade of the 19th century the rush to the Southwest slackened and with it the demand for negroes. The price of slaves reached its highest point in 1818 and had noticeably receded since. On the floor of the Convention gentlemen bewailed this loss. One had in 1817 sold eighty-five slaves averaging $300 apiece, but at the moment it was his firm belief that a similar lot would not bring more than $150 a head. The slump in prices was also reflected in the sums the State paid for slaves executed or sold by it for transportation beyond the limits of the United States. In 1820 the State paid $12,810 for twenty-five negroes, averaging $512.25 each. Ten years later twenty-four cost $8,875 or $369.78 a head. But though he was worth less in the market, the slave could feel more secure in the bosom of his family.

When the usual flood of momentous petitions, such as that of the town of Union praying that hogs be permitted to run at large therein,[4] had been

[2] *House Journal,* 1831-32, Appendix Document 14. Between September 1910 and 1920, Virginia executed four negroes annually (average) for murder alone. For comparison one must add those executed for other crimes and those given life sentences. (Annual Report of the Board of Directors of the Penitentiary.)

[3] Revised Code of 1819, I, 427.

[4] *House Journal,* 1827-28, p. 42.

weathered, the Assembly of 1827-28 took the slave code under consideration. A resolution was adopted declaring it expedient that negroes " emancipated for general and long continued good conduct and character " be granted permission to remain in the State and to abolish the requisite of unanimity upon the part of the judges granting permits. Though a good start, nothing came of it.

Cruelty upon the part of masters was discountenanced by the best of society and punished by law. A reward offered by the Governor in 1828 for the capture of Isham W. Clements witnessed that the law was vigorously enforced. At the coroner's inquest on the body of a woman named Rachel, it appeared that she came to her death by excessive whipping administered by her master, Isham Clements. The master absconded, in consequence of which Governor Giles offered a reward of two hundred dollars for his capture and incarceration in the jail of Goochland County.[5]

A similar offence in 1830 was followed by a similar proclamation offering one hundred dollars for the capture of the felon. Had the slaves run away their masters would hardly have offered more than twenty dollars for their apprehension. These proclamations by the Governor do not comport with the allegation of rabid abolitionists that slaves were murdered with impunity.

[5] *Richmond Enquirer,* December 27, 1828.

In the awakened sensitiveness to the suffering of the unfortunates of society, the free negroes found a champion in no less a personage than Governor Giles. To drive them from Virginia and to hold those permitted to remain under strict rule, their conduct had been seriously limited and the slightest felony punished with great rigor. Upon the statute book they were discriminated against. All too frequently they were punished with a cruelty far exceeding the deserts of their crimes. Between 1823 and 1827 forty-four negroes were sold as '' transports '' in punishment for grand larceny, larceny, infanticide, theft, rape, burglary, horse-stealing, stabbing, murder, malicious shooting, manslaughter, and the theft of one hog.[6]

In his Message to the 1827-28 session of the General Assembly, Giles protested against the cruelty and injustice of a code that would damn a woman and her descendants to perpetual slavery for the theft of a hog.

The propriety and wisdom of depriving one of his liberty in consequence of his crime against society none questioned. But according to every just rule for apportioning punishment to crime, slavery, a punishment of the highest order, should follow crimes of the greatest offence. Yet further injustice resulted because of the indiscriminate meting of this punishment to both sexes. With male offenders the

[6] *House Journal*, 1827-28, Appendix, *Governor's Message and Accompanying Documents*, pp. 23, 24.

punishment terminated with the guilty. With the female punishment passed to their innocent offspring. Though in no wise participators with their mothers in crime, they shared with them in punishment in perpetuity. Such a condition Giles thought " incompatible with every principle of morality and justice and directly repugnant to the just, humane, and liberal policy of Virginia in the dispensation of criminal justice upon every other occasion." He, therefore, recommended the penal code to the attention of the Assembly.

The Governor's words fell upon open ears and willing minds. February 12 witnessed the passage of an act discontinuing the punishment of free negroes by stripes and sale and transportation.[7] A great gain was theirs in the substitution of confinement in the penitentiary with a maximum of eighteen years for the first offense. Even for further offense the sentence could be augmented only to life imprisonment. For the benefit of offenders not disposed of at the time of the passage of the act, judges before whom they were tried were permitted with the consent of the prisoners to commute their sentences to the punishment prescribed by the new act.

Though the reorganization of the judicial system was the major matter before the 1830-31 session, the negro problem was not to be forgotten. There was much yet in the criminal code that was hard and de-

[7] *Acts of The General Assembly*, 1827-28, pp. 29, 30.

manded revision. The House of Delegates took another forward step in ordering a bill to prohibit
burning in the hand " in all cases whatsoever." [8]
In the same spirit the legislature relinquished to the
free negroes, Jacob Sampson and his wife, the estate
of her father, escheated to the State because of her
illegitimacy.

In the light of an event of the preceding January
the House of Delegates ordered the committee for
Courts of Justice to review the law touching the residence of free negroes and to consider " what amendments are necessary . . . . for the suppression of
schools in which free negroes, mulattoes, and slaves
are taught reading and writing." [9] On the recommendation of this committee the House passed, February 24, a bill rigidly circumscribing the free blacks.
With slight modifications the bill passed the Senate
by the close vote of 16 to 15 [10] and became law
April 7, 1831.

The outstanding feature of the bill was the ban
on education. All meetings of free negroes in schools,
churches, meeting-houses, or " any other place by
day or night " in which they shall be taught " under
whatsoever pretext " were forbidden under penalty
of corporal punishment not exceeding twenty lashes.
Whites assembling with them for the purpose of
teaching them were liable to a fine of fifty dollars and

[8] *House Journal*, 1830-31, p. 64.
[9] Ibid., p. 30.
[10] *Senate Journal*, 1830-31, p. 130.

imprisonment not exceeding two months. Whites teaching slaves for pay, or hiring teachers for that purpose, were enjoined to quit this iniquitous practice under pain of a fine of not less than ten nor more than one hundred dollars.[11]

Free negroes continuing to dwell in the State without permission were to be taken up after twelve months and sold by the sheriff into slavery.

The lower counties, after all the fears expressed in the Convention, must have been surprised by the new revenue act. The Finance Committee, in view of the contemplated surplus of seventy-four thousand dollars,[12] recommended a reduction of taxes on horses, slaves, and law processes. Their recommendation was followed and the slave tax accordingly reduced to twenty-five cents upon able-bodied slaves above the age of twelve years.[13]

To paint the bright side is to create but half a portrait. From the gilt and braid in the foreground let us turn to the grovelling figures in the shadows. While the whites were growing more generous in their relations with the lower race, there was a restless, rumbling uneasiness erupting from time to time in insubordination and threatened revolt. Quiet since the Gabriel fright of 1801, the negroes were less and less feared. As the danger was forgotten

[11] *Acts of The General Assembly,* 1830-31, pp. 107, 108.
[12] *House Journal,* 1830-31, p. 289.
[13] *Acts of The General Assembly,* 1830-31, p. 125. The tax had been thirty-five cents. (*Acts of the Assembly,* 1829-30, p. 3.)

the enforcement of the law lagged. But even while
the Convention met there were ominous rumblings
that should have put the government on the watch.

In 1828 a posse, attracted by their bold action, cap-
tured two negroes who had sustained themselves for
eight months by pillaging the country-side and relieving negroes passing after dark of their belong-
ings, some women generously contributing the skirts
they wore.[14] Greater disturbance the next summer
was reflected in the Governor's Message. " A spirit
of dissatisfaction and insubordination was mani-
fested by the slaves in different parts of the country
from this place [Richmond] to the seaboard." [15] A
few negroes were arrested and brought to the Capital. Arms were sent to local volunteer companies, but
happily nothing came of it.

New Year's Day, 1830, had scarcely passed when
one David Walker, a free person of color, found himself in a quandary. In his possession, addressed to
Thomas Seivis, were thirty incendiary pamphlets
calculated to warm the heart of the coldest and most
enervated slave. But, alas and alack, the said Seivis
was dead. In his distress Walker turned for guidance to a white gentleman of the city. The gentleman, " presuming them to be of the class of fanatical
tracts upon the subject of religion," advised him to

[14] *Constitutional Whig*, Nov. 1, 1828.
[15] *House Journal*, 1829-30, p. 8.

put them into circulation without reading them. Unfortunately, the Mayor of Richmond did not approve. In consequence Walker was taken up.[16]

The Governor's Council, upon receiving news of the matter and one of the tracts, advised that the whole affair be brought to the notice of the legislature and attention called to the propriety of amending the law the more thoroughly to prevent " the introduction and circulation of papers, writings, or publications, and for the prohibition of pictures designed . . . . to produce insurrection or insubordination amongst the people of color." [17]

The House of Delegates responded with a bill to suppress " seditious writings " and to prevent the instruction of slaves. The Senate was not yet ready for such drastic measures and considered the bill but two days, postponing it indefinitely, by a vote of 11 to 7.[18] " The severity attempted, defeated any new provision." [19] But, as we saw, the following session brought together an Assembly ready and eager to cope with the abolitionists of the North. The result of their labors we have reviewed.[19a]

Though the States beyond the Potomac had relatively small numbers of negroes, they were not un-

[16] *MSS. Executive Communications,* 1830-35, Archives, Virginia State Library, Richmond, Va.

[17] *MS. Advice Council, Seditious Pamphlet,* Jan. 5, 1830, *Executive Papers, Giles,* 1830, January 1–March 31, Archives.

[18] *Senate Journal,* 1829-30, p. 114.

[19] *Daily Richmond Whig,* Feb. 24, 1830.

[19a] See above, p. 52.

interested in movements looking to the improvement of the lot of the negro. Before the dawn of the nineteenth century societies had come into existence for the purpose of preserving the rights of the freedman, and, as we have already seen, Northern philanthropy played an important part in establishing the American Colonization Society. But with the passage of time, the desire to better the lot of the negro was insidiously warped until abolition, rather than colonization or the preservation of his new-found rights, became the paramount object of agitation. This process was slow and almost imperceptible, but by 1830 the tendency was easily recognized. Advocates of abolition increased in number and noisy denunciation, while friends of colonization failed to keep pace.

The change in objective was accompanied by change in leadership and method. Prominent among the leaders of the Society were such men as Monroe, Madison, Marshall, Clay, and Bushrod Washington. The body of the organization was largely composed of well-to-do property owners. Funds were secured by voluntary gifts. To the generosity of the slaveholder appeal was made both for support and for candidates for colonization. His property was in no wise threatened nor was any attempt made to jeopardize his home and life. With the rise of the abolitionists,—Tappan, Thompson, and Garrison,— all this was changed. From the leadership of the honored and trusted citizens, one steps down to professional agitators with little property to lose and much notoriety to gain. For the appeal to the master they substituted " a course of abuse . . . . which they know must and which they intend shall irritate and madden him. They cherish no object which requires the assent of the slaveholder; they expect to urge the North into measures to coerce abolition, and failing that to incite the negroes to insurrection." [20]

The early leaders were ill received by their countrymen who appreciated the dangers of the scheme they advocated, " a scheme which," in the language of a contemporary, " but a few years since found our country united, tranquil, and happy, and which in that brief period, has planted in her bosom distrust, jealousy, rage, and terror,—which has endangered the industry of the North, the security of life in the South, and has shaken to its very center the Government of our common country." [21] Lundy, editor of the Genius of Universal Emancipation, was publicly denounced in contemporary periodicals. Garrison was lead with a rope through the streets of Boston, and but for the action of a few gentlemen might have received precipitously the excellent suit of tar and feathers generously prepared for him by the mob. Two years later another journalist disciple of abolition, Elijah P. Lovejoy, lost his life at the

[20] Williams, J., *The South Vindicated,* p. 106.
[21] Ibid., p. 150.

hands of a mob infuriated by the terms of oppro-
brium so generously heaped upon the heads of slaveholders.

The Southern States, threatened with insurrection, took energetic measures to prevent the circulation of ''inflammatory pamphlets which the meek and
charitable of other States have seen cause to distribute as firebrands in the bosom of our society.'' [22]
Laws were passed to perpetuate the ignorance of the
blacks and the introduction of incendiary tracts was
made a high crime. Rigid regulatory acts took the
place of charitable amendments to the penal code.
Auxiliary to legal agencies, Vigilance Associations
ferreted out undesirable visitors from the North.

As a result of the campaign of abuse, the mental
attitude of Virginia and the other Southern States
changed. Hitherto public discussion of slavery had
been banned and the system deprecated as an evil
to be deplored and ameliorated as rapidly as the
means at hand would permit. For a brief moment
following the Southampton tragedy the ban was
lifted. Thrown on the defense by the abuse of abolitionists, Southern leaders prepared arguments exculpating the South of blame. From this to the support of the institution was a short step. Even as
late as January 14, 1832,[23] a member of the House of

---

[22] *Journal House of Delegates*, 1831-32, p. 10.

[23] The Speech of Charles Jas. Faulkner (of Berkeley), in the *House
of Delegates of Virginia*, p. 20. This speech is reported to have been
delivered on January 20, but internal evidence and the *House Journal*
point to January 14 as the more probable date.

Delegates was able to express his felicity that none had arisen to defend slavery *per se,* but before the end of that memorable session Professor Dew of William and Mary College had started upon the preparation of arguments propounding the justice and economic soundness of the institution and the utter ruin which was sure to follow its abolition.

In 1831 occurred phenomena of nature which were not without influence in precipitating upon Southampton County a " massacre than which for the narrow bounds of space and time to which it was confined none ever was more indiscriminate, ruthless, and abominable." [24] On February 12 the negroes were not a little disturbed by an eclipse of the sun. On August 12, 13, and 14 the peculiar appearance of the sun again turned their thoughts to religious channels:

On the 12th its [the sun's] appearance was not so extraordinary as on the two following days. On the morning of the 13th, the rays of the sun were an uncommon bluish hue, which continued, with some increase throughout the day; and as he ascended his circuit in the heavens, his face assumed a more than ordinary dazzling brilliance, which gradually disappeared with his declination in the afternoon; and from 5 to 6 o'clock, P. M. it was as placid as that of the " silver Queen of night"; during which period, a dark spot on his disk, inclining to the south was visible to the naked eye . . . . our ebony friends were especially annoyed, and many no doubt, fortunately for themselves, had their religious devotion sensibly stimulated.[25]

[24] *The Letter of Appomattox to The People of Virginia,* p. 4.
[25] *Constitutional Whig,* August 22, 1831.

To Nat, sometimes called Nat Turner, these phenomena were signs from Heaven calling him to take up arms and deliver his people from bondage.

Nat was born the property of Samuel Turner October 2, 1800, five days before the execution of Gabriel and five months after the birth of John Brown who was to make the last attempt to incite a slave insurrection in Virginia. Nat, delicate in childhood, was excused from some of the heavy work of the fields. In his leisure he early learned to read and to pore over his Bible. It was not long before he came to have great influence over his fellows and was thought by some to be a prophet.

His religious bent proved his undoing. Brooding over the lot of his people and encouraged by their homage, he came to regard himself as one chosen of God to do a mighty work. As early as 1825 he had visions. The heavens thundered, white and black spirits fought, and a voice called him to take up his cross. Until a sign should tell him that the hour was at hand he was bidden to be quiet. He accepted the eclipse as that sign. To stir him from his lethargy came the wonders of August.

A feast for a few slaves was arranged for Sunday night, August 21. About three in the morning Nat joined them around their camp fire. A short time passed and then, with seven followers, Nat proceeded to the murder of his master and the latter's stepfather, Joseph Travis.

Seizing horses and arms as they went and gathering some three score adherents, the murderers ran wild through the unfortunate county. None among the whites were spared. But their course was short. There was no general uprising. A repulse during the first day caused them to retrace their steps. The whites speedily armed. An attack upon the home of Dr. Blunt was repulsed with the aid of faithful blacks and the rebellion subsided almost immediately. Nat escaped capture until October 30. He was tried shortly thereafter and hanged on the eleventh of November.[26]

The Southampton Insurrection, short though it was, focussed in awful and violent manner the attention of the entire nation upon the system of slavery. Throughout the country spread a spirit of sympathy for the afflicted county. But some there were who, regretting that the late insurgents had murdered women and children, approved their attempt and sympathized with those about to be hanged.[27] In a current issue of the *African Centinel and Journal of Liberty,* one writer expressed the

[26] There was incarcerated in an asylum in 1900 a negro related to Nat. Like Nat, this one, Hack Brown, was affected along religious lines. To questions asked him, he would reply " So saith the Lord." (William S. Drewry, *The Southampton Insurrection,* p. 28.)

[27] Not the least notorious among them, John Brown (James Redpath, *The Public Life of Capt. Brown,* p. 105).

hope that the slaves would achieve their freedom in
a more successful conflict with their masters:

The writer of this article is a white man, and a white man
who will never raise his pen, his voice, or his arm to quench
the spirit of liberty in the bosoms either of blacks or whites.
The slaves have a perfect right derived from God Almighty
to their freedom. They have done vastly wrong in the last
insurrection, in killing women and children, but still it
is not to be wondered at. Their struggle for freedom is
the same in principle as the struggle of our fathers in '76.
I hope they may achieve their liberty eventually by fair and
honorable means in a brave and manly conflict with their
masters. In short they should refrain from assailing women
and children, and conduct on the true principles of heroism.
I shall for one, wish them success whenever the battle may
come.[28]

Though he had kept discreet silence upon the
proper basis of representation while the slavery
problem in that guise perplexed gentlemen of the
Convention, Governor Floyd now entered upon a
definite policy. Upon learning of the Insurrection,
he confided to his diary that " This day [Aug. 23]
will be a very noted day in Virginia." [29] Rumors of
insurrections in other counties in no wise cooled his
ardor, while the arrival of a copy of the Liberator
occasioned a statement as to the inevitable disruption of the Union if the people of one section con-

---

[28] *Richmond Enquirer,* Oct. 18, 1831.

[29] " The Diary of John Floyd " in *John P. Branch Historical Papers
of Randolph-Macon College,* ed., Chas. H. Ambler, V. nos. 1 and 2,
p. 151.

tinued unchecked to plot the destruction of those in
another.

On the sixteenth of September, Floyd considered
requiring of the Governor of Massachusetts the
prosecution of Knapp and Garrison. Two days later
the machinations of "conspirators" in Philadelphia caused him to write: "If we to the South ever
feel the influence of their measures, this Union is
at an end . . . . I think I shall be able in the end to
disappoint their plans." [30] On the twenty-first of
November his intention was recorded: "Before I
leave this Government, I will have contrived to have
a law passed gradually abolishing slavery in this
State, or at all events to begin the work by prohibiting slavery on the West side of the Blue Ridge Mountains." [31] Looking ahead to December twenty-sixth
we find:

> The public business gets on slowly. The question of the
> gradual abolition of slavery begins to be mooted. The Eastern
> members, meaning those east of the Blue Ridge Mountains,
> wish to avoid the discussion, but it must come if I can influ-
> ence my friends in the Assembly to bring it on. I will not
> rest until slavery is abolished in Virginia.[32]

After the first fright had subsided, the people of
Virginia broke the ban of repression, pulled the veil
of studied silence from the foul figure of slavery,
and disclosed its horrid features, subjecting it to the
piercing light of examination. Public meetings were

[30] Ibid., p. 161.
[31] Ibid., p. 166.
[32] Ibid., p. 168.

held, articles written for periodicals, petitions circulated, and memorials addressed to the legislature. No longer did one breathe the name of slavery in whispers, but boldly at every opportunity made it the subject of heated discussion and debate. Everywhere arose the sound of voices, some denouncing slavery, others defending it, but above the din was heard the clear call, " Something must be done." Upon the General Assembly soon to meet every eye turned for the answer to that cry.

CHAPTER IV

The Slavery Debate in the General Assembly, 1831-32

To the General Assembly the State turned for relief from the danger of such outrages as so recently had wet her soil with blood. While some demanded the abolition of slavery and others the revision and strengthening of the militia, the fervent hope and acute interest of all brought the discussion in the legislature, in an unwonted degree, into the homes and lives of the people.

The members of this notable session of the General Assembly had unfortunately been elected without reference to this most pressing question. Even the new members had campaigned on other issues and achieved success months before Nat projected slavery into the limelight of political attention. Though the Assembly was lacking in an expression of the will of their constituents upon this issue, it was not lacking in ability. The older leaders of the Convention had passed, giving place to that younger group we noticed above. Nature, association with the patriarchs of a former day, and experience combined to fit them for the momentous task. Chief among them were James McDowell, soon to be governor and congressman, Charles Faulkner, later

minister to Paris and member of Jackson's staff,
and William B. Preston, before long congressman
and Secretary of the Navy under Taylor. Upon William O. Goode devolved the leadership of the pro-
slavery forces.

The Assembly convened December 5. Speakers
and clerks having been elected, Governor Floyd's
Message was read. It was in part as follows:

Fellow-Citizens of the Senate and the House of Delegates:

You are again assembled under circumstances calculateu
to inspire the community with a just expectation, that your
deliberations, will be followed by measures equal in energy
and decision to the crisis in which your country is placed.
. . . . occurrences of a grave and distressing character which
have taken place since your adjournment . . . . cause the
people to turn their eyes upon you at this time with profound
and fixed attention . . . .

The most active among ourselves in stirring up the spirit
of revolt have been the negro preachers. They had acquired
great ascendency over the minds of their fellows and . . . .
prepared them for the development of the final design. . . . .
There is also . . . . reason to believe those preachers have
. . . . been the channels through which the inflammatory
papers and pamphlets brought here by the agents and emissaries from other States, have been circulated amongst our
slaves. The facilities thus afforded for plotting treason and
conspiracy to rebel and make insurrection, have been great.
Through the indulgence of the magistracy and the laws, large
collections of slaves have been permitted to take place at any
time through the week for the ostensible purpose of indulging
in religious worship. . . . . The sentiments and sometimes
the words of these inflammatory pamphlets which the meek
and charitable of other States have seen cause to distribute

as firebrands in the bosom of our society, have been read. What shall be thought of those friends, who, having no interest in our community nevertheless, seek to excite a servile war; a war, which exhausts itself in the massacre of unoffending women and children on the one side and on the other, in the sacrifice of all who have borne part in the savage undertaking? Not only should the severest punishment be inflicted upon those disturbers of our peace, whenever they or their emissaries are found within our reach, but decisive measures should be adopted to make all their measures abortive. The public good requires the negro preachers be silenced, who full of ignorance are incapable of inculcating anything but notions of the wildest superstition, thus preparing fit instruments in the hands of the crafty agitators, to destroy the public tranquillity.

As the means of guarding against the possible repetition of these sanguinary scenes, I cannot fail to recommend to your early attention, the revision of all the laws intended to preserve in due subordination, the slave population of our State.[1]

In addition to the regular Committee for Courts of Justice, Linn Banks, Speaker of the House, appointed a Committee on the Coloured Population.[2] The latter was not long without work, for Miers W. Fisher of Northampton immediately proposed that

[1] *Journal of House of Delegates,* 1831-32, pp. 8 et seq.

[2] For a complete list of the Assembly see the Appendix.

The first committee was composed of William H. Brodnax, Bryce, Goode, Moore, George I. Williams, Gholson, John C. Campbell, John G. Williams, Faulkner, Newton, Daniel, Wilson of Botetourt, and John Chandler. (*House Journal,* p. 8.) The Coloured Population Committee consisted of Brodnax, Fisher, Cobb, Wood of Albemarle, Roane, Moore, J. C. Campbell, Gholson, Stillman, Newton, Smith of Frederick, Brown and Anderson of Nottoway. (*House Journal,* p. 15.)

so much of the Governor's Message as concerned
slaves and free negroes be referred to it.

Constantly during the first months the House was
receiving petitions concerning the colored population. Laying aside private positions and reserving
for later consideration those praying that free
negroes be prohibited from working under certain
conditions, there remains a group urging the legislature to take steps to dissipate the black menace.
All the petitioners called attention to the pressing
need of banishing the free negro and many desired
that some effective system of reducing the number
of slaves be adopted. Not a few suggested that the
whole matter of the blacks should be handled by the
United States. The petition of the citizens of Fauquier County is most typical:

The undersigned inhabitants of the County of Fauquier
respectfully declare that they believe that the time has arrived
when it is highly expedient that the Government of the
United States should possess the power to raise and appropriate money for the purpose of transporting free persons of
color to the coast of Africa, that it should also possess the
power to purchase slaves and transport them likewise.

Therefore they petition the Legislature to take early and
effectual measures to effect an amendment to the Constitution
of the United States, that will enable the Congress of the
United States to pass the necessary laws to effect the above
specified objects.[3]

In other petitions the State was urged to act, re-
lying upon its own resources, for " it is most clear

[3] *MS. Petitions to the General Assembly,* 1831, Fauquier, December
7, Archives, Virginia State Library, Richmond, Va.

that . . . . the public interests and safety of individuals call aloud for . . . . the ultimate removal of a race so irreconcilably antagonistic to ours." [4] From Leesburg in Loudoun County came a demand for the abolition of slavery based on three propositions fully proved by sad experience. In that community slave labor was the most expensive one could use. In addition, its use was attended by the destruction of the region that supported it. The third cause of distress was the apprehension and fear of attack, driving peace from the bosom of all. [5]

If the head of man be impervious to reason, perhaps the tender voice from Augusta may melt the heart:

Although it be unexampled in our beloved state that females should interfere in its political concerns, and although we feel all the timidity incident in our sex, in taking this step, ... we pretend not to conceal from you our fathers and brothers, our protectors . . . . the fears whch agitate our bosoms, and the dangers which await us, as revealed to us by recent tragical deeds. Our fears we admit are great; we do not concede that they spring from the superstitious timidity of our sex. Alas we are indeed timid; but we appeal to your manly reason, to your more mature wisdom to attest the justice & propriety of our fears, when we call to your remembrance the late slaughter of our sisters & their little ones in certain parts of our land & the strong probability that that slaughter was but a partial execution of a widely projected scheme of carnage. We do not, we cannot know the night, nor the unguarded moment, by day or by night which

[4] *MS. Petitions to the General Assembly,* 1831, Loudoun, December 23.

[5] Ibid.

is pregnant with our destruction, that of our husbands, &
brothers & sisters, & children; but we do know that we are
at every moment, exposed to the means of our own excision
& of all that is dear to us in life. The bloody monster which
threatens us is warmed & cherished on our own hearths.
O hear our prayers & remove it, ye protectors of our persons,
ye guardians of our peace . . . . we implore you by the
urgency of our fears, by the love we bear you as our fathers
& brothers, by our anxieties for the little ones around us, by
our estimate of domestic weal, by present danger, by the
prospect of the future, by our female virtues, by the patriotism
which animates & glows in our bosoms, by our prayers to
Almightly God.[6]

If a spur were needed to keep the legislators at
their work, the interest, hopes, and fears of their constituents served adequately. On what few days he did
not witness the presentation of a petition, the delegate had but to look at the newspapers to have his
attention drawn to the one engrossing subject. The
papers filled with letters, editorials, and long ex-
tracts of speeches made in the House, played a most
important part both in exerting influence upon the
delegates and in molding the opinion of their constituents.

December 12 witnessed the commencement of the
long struggle between the abolitionists and their
pro-slavery opponents. The former, strengthened
by the arrival of sundry petitions, were ready to
open manœuvers. On the motion of George Summers, of Kanawha, resolutions were adopted re-

[6] *MS. Petitions to the General Assembly,* 1832, Augusta, January
19.

questing the senate to lay before the house what it
possessed of the correspondence between James
Monroe and Thomas Jefferson relative to colonization. On motion of William C. Rives the colored
population committee took under consideration the
propriety of devoting to colonization such funds as
should accrue to the State in consequence of claims
upon the United States.[7]

Two days later William H. Roane presented petitions from the Society of Friends and the citizens
of Hanover County which were, by accident, to occasion the first great debate. The Friends were certain that the present difficulties were but the inevitable results of the original departure from the
Law of Justice and Humanity fixed by the Creator
for the regulation of his subjects in their dealings
one with another. Founded in injustice, the present
relation of the white to the black man must be completely abandoned before the difficulties perplexing
the public mind would vanish. Nothing short of
abolition could heal the injustice done the negroes
and save the Commonwealth. As the most expeditious means of effecting so desirable an end, the
Friends would call the attention of the legislature to
the wisdom of declaring free all negroes born after
a given date. Supplementary to this program Vir-

[7] *House Journal*, 1831-32, p. 25. Declared by the Governor to be
" near a million dollars." (*Diary of John Floyd,* p. 170.)

6

ginia alone, or in conjunction with the United States, should acquire territory for their settlement.[8]

After disclaiming any intention of discussing the means by which slavery was fastened upon the country, the petitioners from Hanover presented an illuminating table showing the relative strength of the white and black population east of the Blue Ridge.[9]

Census of	Whites	Blacks	Majority of Whites	Majority of Blacks	Gain of Blacks
1790	314,523	289,425	25,098		
1800	336,389	339,393	....	3,004	28,102
1810	338,553	386,942	....	48,389	45,385
1820	348,873	413,928	....	65,055	16,666
1830	375,935	457,013	....	81,078	16,023

106,176

In view of these figures one could hardly expect less than a considerable gain in favor of the blacks at the end of forty years. Anticipating this condition, already many of the more industrious and enterprising, hence more desirable, people of Hanover had settled their affairs and moved, that they and their posterity might not know the dangers of suspended or active insurrection. Many there were who, did the State but offer means of transportation, would gladly have divested themselves of such dangerous property. To this end let but a slight tax be put upon the blacks, free as well as slave, and the " most happy and salutary effects " would follow, presaging a " final and full triumph over all difficulties."

[8] *MS. Petitions to the General Assembly,* 1831, Charles City, December 14.

[9] *Petitions to the General Assembly,* 1831, Hanover, December 14.

Unacquainted with the nature of the petitions and desirous of saving time, William O. Goode moved their reference to the proper committee. Vincent Witcher, ere long to gain notoriety because of his tireless obstruction, disclosed their nature and demanded that if the motion stood, it should be made a test vote and the ayes and nays be recorded. Enlightened by the reading, Goode withdrew his motion and moved instead that they be rejected, warning against consideration of such issues. Were the legislature to become an open forum for the discussion of the dangers of slavery and plans for emancipation, repetition of the Southampton tragedy on an augmented scale might be expected. A false impression would arise that the fright pervading the State was more general and acute than every one knew it to be. Might not one believe the legislature of Virginia moved by its fears? Did anyone suppose that news of this talk of emancipation would fail to reach the ears of the slaves? If the African population for a moment thought the legislature driven to this pass by the murders of August, there would be generated an uneasiness and restlessness productive of the greatest evil.[10]

Charles Carter opposed reference on the grounds that the committee was raised to deal with free negroes and would be swamped by the addition of the slavery issues. Samuel Moore thought a message from so respectable a body demanded proper

[10] *Constitutional Whig,* Dec. 17, 1831.

hearing. While not disposed to hamper the committee in the handling of the free negroes, he believed it was called upon to consider " another and greater nuisance,—slavery itself." [11] Any plan likely to accomplish this would receive his support. Williams, of Harrison, assured the House that upon this important topic the West would give the East " a *carte blanche,* with the sincere hope that some efficient measure might be adopted, towards which they (Western Members) would give their most hearty co-operation." [12] J. Thompson Brown, though decrying any possibility of bettering conditions, invited the presentation of petitions of every kind. When every man with a plan had been heard, when the whole wisdom of the State had labored and shed its full light upon the tangled problems, the legislature could act with authority, and whatever it did would be definitive, the people would be satisfied and feel that this question had been settled " finally and forever." [13] To Chandler, the day that witnessed the deliverance of Virginia from the curse of slavery would be the most glorious since the Fourth of July, 1776.

Under the pressure of general opposition, Goode limited his motion to the Quakers' petition. In the signal defeat of his motion, 93 to 27, the House [14] reaffirmed in unquestionable manner the right of the

[11] *Richmond Enquirer,* December 17, 1831.
[12] Ibid.
[13] Ibid.
[14] *House Journal,* 1831-32, p. 29.

people to have petitions respectfully considered. For the next four weeks the struggle over abolition was restricted to the committee room, but on January 11 Goode forced the House into an acrid debate. The local press, he declared, was committing great injury to property and the safety of society. Unable to hear the debates themselves, subscribers received a false impression as to the probability of the adoption of any measure looking toward abolition. Already the value of slaves had taken a great drop in anticipation of emancipation so boldly proclaimed by local editors. In the breasts of the slaves was raised and nourished the expectation of legislative action. Did the legislature take action, well and good, but if no plan were adopted, great and bitter would be the disappointment felt by them. How easy then for a Nat Turner to arise in every county and fan smouldering passions into flame. He therefore conjured the House " by its respect for public tranquillity—for the rights of property—by humanity, for it was inhuman to inspire hopes in slaves which could never be realized—to arrest a state of things productive of so much alarm, pain and injury " [15] and to adopt his resolution:

Resolved, That the select committee raised on the subject of slaves, free negroes and the melancholy occurrences growing out of the tragical massacre in Southampton, be discharged from the consideration of all petitions, memorials, and resolutions, which have for their object the manumission of persons

[15] *Constitutional Whig,* Jan. 17, 1832.

held in servitude under the existing laws of the commonwealth, and that it is not expedient to legislate on the
subject.[16]

Thomas Jefferson Randolph accepted the challenge and moved that the resolution be amended by
excising all after the word " Southampton " and
substituting therefor:

be instructed to enquire into the expediency of submitting
to the vote of the qualified voters the propriety of providing
by law, that the children of all female slaves who may be
born in this state on or after the fourth day of July, 1840,
shall become the property of the commonwealth, the males
at the age of twenty-one years, the females at the age of
eighteen if detained by their owners within the limits of
Virginia until they shall respectively arrive at the ages aforesaid; to be hired out until the net sum arising therefrom shall
be sufficient to defray the expenses of their removal beyond
the limits of the United States.[17]

The issue being joined the parties proceeded to
one of the most acute and sustained debates ever
heard in that hall. Moore charged slavery, " the
heaviest calamity which has ever befallen any portion of the human race," with the destruction of
every semblance of virtue and morality. The boon
companion of slavery, ignorance, rendered it unprin-
cipled. The slave could not appreciate moral principles, judge of the enormity of crime, or partake of
the satisfaction consequent to creditable deeds.
Possessed of no property, he could have none of the

[16] *Journal of the House of Delegates,* 1831-32, p. 93.
[17] Ibid.

incentive of the free man to labor. On the contrary, his passions and fears were his law, and the likelihood of detection the measure of his criminal activity. Herded together, improperly housed, irregularities of a sexual nature were the rule. The large mulatto population witnessed the all too common illicit relations of the whites with their degraded subject people.

As a brake upon the growth of the white rural population, slavery kept the country the poorer, for it was upon the former that the prosperity of the State chiefly rested. Another consequence of the black man occupying the place of the white was the lessened ability of the State to defend itself in case of war. What would be the attitude of the blacks in this contingency none could say. But granted that they were quiet, the ability of the State to defend itself was impaired to the full measure of their number.

The next day James H. Gholson, of Brunswick, addressed the House in support of Goode's resolution. After voicing his regrets that this topic had been so widely aired, he settled down to an attack on Randolph's amendment. The rights of property holders were guaranteed by both the Virginia and the United States constitutions, the fifth article of the amendments to the latter declaring: " nor shall private property be taken for public use without just compensation." To submit to the electorate the question of abolishing slavery would be to jeopardize the title to this property and therefore cause a depreciation in its value. Neither the people themselves nor their representatives had the right to confiscate property without compensation. Compensation was entirely beyond the realm of the possible.

That the State, though unable to invalidate the title to property existing, was competent to destroy that to property unborn, was a sophism in which he and his constituents took little stock. Did anyone question the title of the farmer to the fruits of his orchard? Could anyone deprive him of colts born of his mares? In equal security could he not claim children born of his slaves?

Regard for the States to the South should give Virginia pause. Measures of so great import as Virginia was debating should be taken only after consultation with the other members of the Union, for they were concerned. The prosperity and happiness of Virginia was not alone at stake. Undigested action would bring ruin to her neighbors likewise.

Only upon the grounds of public safety would Gholson go an inch in support of abolition. If it were proved that slavery threatened the existence of society, with the cry " *Salus populi suprema est lex* " upon his lips, would he rush to the aid of his native State.

Rives denied that one might attribute the present discussion solely to the late massacre. That bloody tragedy was but the realization of long standing apprehension. That the fear of such was a thing of years the statute books witnessed with constantly recurring militia, patrol, and police acts. Why the attempt to perpetuate the ignorance of the slaves but for the fear of insurrection? No, Virginia had but experienced earlier than expected an event constantly feared. Since the cause of this melancholy occurrence was not removed with its suppression, it behooved the legislature to consider this problem fully.

On January 13 [18] General Brodnax took up, one after the other, the manifold attacks leveled at the slaveholder and the " peculiar institution." This form of property, regardless of the manner of acquisition in the first instance, was held in as clear title as that to horses and cattle. But clear as was the title, it was all too evident that the African was a source of danger to the peace and security of society. Only upon the manner of remedy could there be any division. Two means presented themselves; removal of the blacks or the most horrible of servile wars and massacres.

To be successful, any scheme of abolition had of necessity to be founded upon three axiomatic principles: no emancipation without deportation, security of property, and consent of the owner. The first principle he found the constant practice of the Assembly. Only by special license were free negroes allowed to remain in Virginia.

[18] Incorrectly reported in *Richmond Enquirer*, January 24, 1832, and contemporary pamphlets as of January 19. Close study of the *House Journal* and the pamphlets, and the *Richmond Enquirer* for January 14 and 24 show it to have been delivered January 13.

Any proposal that failed to consider the will of masters or trenched upon the sacred rights of property would defeat itself. Violent reaction would follow its initiation and the work of relieving the commonwealth be retarded. Adhering strictly to the second principle, Brodnax could but oppose Randolph's amendment for it contained a twofold attack on property. The very act of submitting to the electorate the question of declaring free the *post nati* would cause a depreciation of slave values. To such partial confiscation he could never consent. By what right could the non-slaveholder claim to decide the disposition of this property? He was no more competent to act in this matter than a third self-appointed party in a civil affair. The greatest loss would occur because of the confiscation of the *post nati*. Not only would the infants be lost but the value of their mothers would sink immediately upon the adoption of such a proposal. Instead of a title in fee simple, possession would become but life interest.

What then was the supreme obstacle to abolition? The one paramount obstacle was the magnitude of the undertaking. According to the census of 1830, Virginia, with less than one-fifteenth of the white population of the United States, supported more than one-seventh of the free negroes and one-fifth of the slaves. This State alone had seventy-five times as many slaves as all the States north of Maryland,[19] more than Louisiana and South Carolina combined, more than Louisiana, Mississippi, Alabama, and Tennessee lumped together. As early as 1803 there were more free negroes and mulattoes in Virginia than in Massachusetts, Maine, New Hampshire, Rhode Island, Connecticut, and Vermont, yet this class had increased rapidly to the total of 47,048. To the 416,350 slaves east of the Blue Ridge there must be added 53,488 beyond. While the annual increase of the slaves was but 4,500, the free blacks added 1,100 to their number.

The mere purchase of 470,000 slaves at the average value of two hundred dollars would entail the expenditure of $94,000,000. To this add $15,000,000 to cover colonization charges. The sum of these placed alongside of the assessed value of land and houses, $206,000,000,[20] at once revealed the impossibility of successfully prosecuting such a program.

Granted that no new influence acted upon the increase of the negroes, they would in a few decades be so strong numerically as to threaten the very existence of the whites. Brodnax thought the situation imperiously demanded heroic action. "Unless something is done in time to obviate it, the day must arrive when scenes of inconceivable horror must inevitably occur, and one of these two races of human

---

[19] *A Century of Population Growth,* pp. 80, 133. See also Dew, Thomas R., *Pro-Slavery Argument,* p. 446, note.

The Argument is essentially the *Review of the Debate in the Virginia Legislature,* enlarged.

[20] Ibid., p. 357.

beings will have their throats cut by the other. It is impossible that things can always continue to flow on in their present current without some radical change in our policy toward the African.'' [21]

But as great as was his anxiety to save the State from this dire catastrophe, greater still was his respect for, and love of property. '' Unless some plan can be struct out . . . . consistent with these principles, dreadful as would be the alternative, I will sit down in silent despair and fold my arms with the desperate resolution, of letting the evil roll on to its horrid consummation.''

Through the gloom shone a ray of hope. On every hand were free negroes whose excision could be effected at the sole cost of removal. Here lay the road to salvation. Upon the expediency of removing this class all were agreed. What then should delay the removal of these with all speed? Let down the bars to emancipation and remove those who should be freed for the purpose. Brodnax asserted of his own knowledge that the State need have no fear for lack of emigrants for some years. There would yet remain a large class which might be secured for a small fraction of their value as slaves. Many owners would readily part with their slaves for a small fraction of their value. Finally, the annual purchase of six thousand young and virile blacks would prevent the increase of this race while affording the whites oppor-

[21] *The Speech of William H. Brodnax*, p. 24.

tunity to swell their numbers so that they need never fear the blacks again.

While the House was yet debating Goode's motion, Brodnax reported for the committee. Though the committee had baffled Goode in completing its labors, his feeling aroused by the report must have been that of satisfaction, for the report read:

> The select committee to whom was referred certain memorials praying the passage of some law providing for the gradual abolition of slavery in this commonwealth, have according to order had the same under consideration, and have come to the following resolution thereupon.
>
> *Resolved* as the opinion of this committee, That it is inexpedient for the present to make any legislative enactments for the abolition of slavery.[22]

If he was pleased, his pleasure was almost immediately to undergo serious diminution, for William Preston moved an amendment making it read: "*Resolved* as the opinion of this committee, That it is expedient to adopt some legislative enactments for the abolition of slavery."[23]

Unfortunately many, though personally in favor of abolition, could not adopt any definite program to this end without an unequivocable mandate from their constituents. Archibald Bryce, Powell, and Randolph were among those thus lost, although they hoped some plan of abolition might be adopted in the near future. Randolph, as we saw, suggested

[22] *House Journal*, 1831-32, p. 99.
[23] Ibid., p. 99.

that the matter be referred to the people themselves. Legislative action in accordance with their will could follow at the next session.

The final struggle was largely carried on by Randolph, Bolling, McDowell, Chandler, and Moore on the one side and Goode and Brown on the other. The defence of the latter group rested solely upon the rights of property and in its train the near-impossibility of granting compensation for the confiscation of this wealth. Against these buttresses, Randolph and his group could urge economic and political considerations on the one hand and the *salus populi* on the other. With what degree of deliberation and unity their attacks were planned we cannot know, but it is certain that they followed in a most happy sequence.

On the sixteenth Preston argued that slaves were not property under common law but became so by statutory enactment.[24] Being property under statutory enactment, they might be divested of that character by another act of the same body. On the next day Summers followed Preston's lead. Society protected property subject to the limitation that it promote the general welfare of the community. Whenever it became subversive of that end, society might not only withdraw its protection but order the destruction of the menace. Like the individuals of which it was composed, society had the right and duty of self-preservation.

[24] *Constitutional Whig,* January 28, 1832. See above, p. 2.

Gholson had invoked the Constitution of Virginia in defense of property rights. He would stay the hand of abolitionists. Chandler now called it in to speed the hand of abolitionists. No one proposed confiscating the slaves " for public use." On the contrary, they were to become a charge upon the public. It was a fact of everyday observance that the body politic authorized the destruction of menaces to the safety of its citizens, and that without compensating owners. Did any receive payment for the loss of a tottering building condemned by county or corporation? Under the same right the State could destroy slavery.

Not alone had it the right to act, but it had the duty. In the clause, " That man has certain unalienable rights of which when he enters society he cannot by any compact deprive his posterity: namely the enjoyment of life and liberty," Chandler found a mandate to act. Gholson claimed property in the issue of female slaves *ad infinitum.* Chandler claimed it the duty of the State to protect posterity for an equally long period. Every man was guaranteed the enjoyment of life, liberty, and the pursuit of happiness. For proof of the fact that slavery was incompatible with the full enjoyment of these rights one needed but to look to Southampton. *Salus populi suprema est lex.* Imperious was the call of duty. Fasten not this curse upon posterity.

Brown delivered a lengthy defense of slavery, but offered no constructive criticism except the reforma-

tion of the militia. Randolph's plan came in for a
good drubbing. While offering no relief for twenty-
six years, it was calculated to cause the greatest
unrest with its first application. The slave born prior
to the all important date, July 4, 1840, destined to
life-long servitude, must by nature begrudge his
younger brother the freedom that was his through
the sole merit of being younger. Pondering over his
lot, the elder could not but " regard himself as the
victim of injustice. . . . . cheerfulness and content-
ment will flee from his bosom and the most harm-
less and happy creature that lives on the earth will
be transformed into a dark, designing and desperate
rebel." [25]

Among the ranks of the rebels would be not a few
slaves driven to violence, albeit born in the new dispensation. Did the owner desire to hold his slave in
subjection after becoming of age, he had but to
remove this property beyond the limits of the State.
No one with the slightest knowledge of human nature
could suppose for one moment that the young man
about to receive his freedom would allow himself
to be so cheated without striking a blow for its
achievement.

Shifting his attack, Brown considered Federal aid.
He admitted that it might be got, but at too dear a
price,—partial confiscation and subserviency to the
North. Doubtless Northern congressmen would join
in the undertaking, if for no other reason, because

[25] *The Speech of J. Thompson Brown*, p. 8.

of jealousy. With every diminution of slavery in the South, the power of the North would become relatively stronger in the House of Representatives. A few States purged of this evil and several seats emptied, Congress would sever the Gordian knot with the keen blade of confiscation and exult over the prostrate form of the South. Virginia, debilitated by the diminution of her Representatives, would sink lower in the scale of political importance.

After expatiating upon the impossibility of purchasing and transporting the slaves, Brown entered upon a eulogy of slavery itself only excelled by the forensic flourish of Knox on the preceding day.

Feeling was every day growing more tense and dangerous. Delegates from the Tidewater and the counties to the south of the James River held tenaciously to their property, while gentlemen from the West declared that division of the State would be preferable to union only to be overwhelmed by the black flood. " If we are to remain united, we must have some guarantee, that the evils under which you labor shall not be extended to us," one of them cried.[26]

At last Randolph spoke in defence of his plan. For twenty-six years the State could be making ready before it would be called upon for the first removal. Three-fourths of the people at the moment living would have died and another generation accustomed to the idea would be almost ready to put it into

[26] *The Speech of Charles J. Faulkner*, p. 8.

7

operation. Ample time would have been afforded for the removal of slaves beyond the borders of the State. Emancipation would slip upon the State without jolt or jostle. For the completion of the work eighty years would be necessary, a period sufficiently long to permit of the substitution of native and immigrant white labor. But happiest of all the execution of the system would not burden the treasury. To the wages of negroes hired out by the sheriff one looked for the revenue required.

In their anxiety gentlemen had seen in this amendment an attack upon property that was in no wise embodied in the draft or necessarily implied in its execution. Indeed the draft left the problem of execution to a future session of the legislature. Randolph believed that the State might expedite matters by purchasing infants to be left with their mothers.[27]

Brodnax had objected to submitting the fate of this property to the electorate. Representation in the House of Delegates, he recalled, had been allotted by the Convention with the deliberate intention of safeguarding property—slave property. The East had not been willing to allow the West to express itself with all the power that it would have were population adopted as the index and basis for political power. The East could not now submit to the

[27] Thomas Jefferson had outlined such a plan for the removal of the after-born of the slaves, and had contemplated payment for infants to be left with their mothers until their labor should have reembursed their mothers' masters. (*Letter to Jared Sparks in H. B. Adams, Jared Adams, I, 252.*)

destruction of the guarantee and compromise agreed on two years before.

Randolph, conceding that the non-slaveholders had no immediate pecuniary interest involved in the fate of slavery, championed their right to partake in such a grave and pregnant decision. If equal liability to public obligation and self-preservation were legitimate grounds, then was their right well established. Were they exempt from patrol duty? Did they not pay taxes for a militia largely directed against, and occasioned by, the slaves of their more propertied brothers? Were not they alike exposed to the fury of insurrection? Nay, was not their safety especially jeopardized by their employment as overseers and agents of punishment?

With a vision almost prophetic, Randolph conjured the House to save the State, for already the hand of fate had written upon the wall:

> There is one circumstance to which we are to look as inevitable in the fulness of time; a dissolution of this Union . . . . and when it does come, border war follows it. . . . . Suppose an invasion by your enemy, in part with black troops, speaking the same language, of the same nation, burning with enthusiasm for the liberation of their race. . . . . Are we prepared to barter the liberty of our children for slaves for them? Is it not wise policy while the evil is still within our grasp; when we can gradually obliterate it, with gentle forbearance to all; while we can still restrain it, by the strong hand of power or crush its movements in blood if necessary, to prepare the way for better prospects to our children, brighter hopes to posterity? [28]

[28] *The Speech of Thomas J. Randolph*, p. 8.

On the following day, January 21, James McDowell occupied the floor for an hour and a half in most puissant fashion arraying the misfortunes consequent upon the existence of the slave system. In remedy he proposed a compromise of the plans sponsored by Brodnax and Randolph. Like the former, he considered the transportation of such slaves as should be voluntarily manumitted for that purpose. Like the latter, he centered the activity of the State upon the *post nati,* but carried this plan a step further than Randolph had dared advocate. While voluntary surrender of the *post nati* was desired, should they be refused, title " should be purchased . . . . but if the State have not the means . . . . then this claim should be forfeited to the State in such manner as shall best preserve the interests of individuals without hazarding too much the interests and safety of the Commonwealth." [29] Like Randolph too, McDowell warned against the dangers of civil war:

Let it not be said . . . . that the dismemberment of these States is a visionary one, an improbable presumption. . . . . It is but too unhappily the contrary. Whether we look to matters of fact or to the results of reasoning, the event adverted to is anything but visionary. No man who looks to the posture or prospects of our federal relations and understands the grounds on which they rest but well knows that this very event at this very hour is lowering over the otherwise sunny face of our national fortunes. No man who sees at all, but must perceive the gathering auguries which premonish us of its approach. And when it does come who can tell

[29] *The Speech of James McDowell,* p. 14.

the political coalitions which may follow it? . . . . One thing we may be said to know. It is this . . . . that the slave-holding interest of the country will and can coalesce with no other interest and must as a consequence be separate and hostile to all others.

The effect of McDowell's speech was indeed flattering. No one raised his voice in opposition. After a short silence, John C. Campbell moved that Goode's resolution and the amendment thereto be laid upon the table. Though the teeth of the resolution had been knocked out by the report of the committee and the continued debate, Campbell's motion was barely able to secure a majority.

All the while the House of Delegates had been watched by a spectator in the executive mansion. Frequent conferences with his diary betrayed the interest with which the governor followed every turn in the struggle for abolition. Some of his inner thoughts we have seen. The early progress of the debate found reflections in daily notations revealing gubernatorial satisfaction. Even so late as the twenty-third, Floyd wrote: " Many speculations are now made upon the result of this debate. We can carry the question, if necessary, by about two votes. . . . . '' [30]

The debate nearing its close, Goode explained the motives that actuated him and threatened division of the State if his advice was not followed:

If gentlemen have not been hurried away by the heat and ardor of debate, if they cherish the fixed, the immutable pur-

[30] " The Diary of John Floyd " in the *Historical Papers of Randolph-Macon College,* ed. Chas. H. Ambler, V, nos. 1 and 2, p. 170.

pose of renewing and pressing the consideration of this subject, then I say there is no hope of peace, except in a division
of this great commonwealth. . . . . If the agitation of the
question be continued I shall in every character which I may
fill, exert myself to produce that division. I shall do so
myself: I shall earnestly recommend it to my constituents.[31]

Jones accepted the challenge and continued the
denunciation of slavery.[32] From the lips of Samuel
McDowell Moore fell a counter threat:

He for one was resolved never to permit the question to rest
as long as slavery continued to exist in the Commonwealth.
He feared that nothing effectual would be done at the present
session, but . . . . felt strong hopes the work of emancipation
would be recommended by the next. . . . . If he should be
there again he would again stir the question as long as he

[31] *Constitutional Whig*, March 28, 1832.
[32] The statement is frequently made, that Virginia took to breeding
slaves. Harold U. Faulkner (*American Economic History*, p. 225),
says: "Selling their surplus slaves, the border States, particularly
Virginia, actively took up the business of slave raising and slave
trading." J. A. Woodburn (*Life of Thaddeus Stevens*, p. 97), quotes
Stevens: "Virginia is now only fit to be the breeder not the em-
ployer of slaves. . . . . Instead of attempting to renovate the soil,
and by their own honest labor compelling the earth to yield her
abundance . . . . the sons of that great state must devote their time
to selecting and grooming the most lusty sires and the most fruitful
wenches to supply the slave barracoons of the South." Another writer
speaks of "nursuries" for the breeding of slaves.
    Winfield H. Collins, in his *Domestic Slave Trade of the Southern
States*, has drawn up a strong argument in refutation from census returns. If the "breeding" States were engaged in breeding slaves the
ratio of the slaves under the age of ten to the whole slave population
in these States should be greater than that in the so-called "buying"
States. But this condition is not found in the census returns; indeed
the average ratio for all the slave States was exactly that of Virginia.
    To account for "nursuries" one need go no further than the
humane treatment accorded pregnant women on large plantations,

should be a member of the Legislature. . . . . He would return to his constituents and advise them never to elect any man who was opposed to it. In fine, he was prepared to recommend to every father, to take his son, (as Hannibal was carried by Hamilcar in olden times) to the altar and swear him never to give up the cause of emancipation until his efforts are crowned with complete success.[33]

On Wednesday, January 25, events moved rapidly to a close. Witcher moved in vain to postpone indefinitely discussion of the subject. Preston's amendment was disposed of by an adverse vote of 58-73.[34] On the motion of Archibald Bryce the House added, 67-60, an amendment making the report read:

The select committee to whom was referred certain memorials praying the passage of a law providing for the gradual

---

and surely none but large plantations could afford to have "nursuries." Women within a month or two of child-birth were not infrequently relieved of heavier work and set to tasks about the "big house." Would it be strange then to find on a plantation of two or three hundred slaves, fifty or sixty of whom were women, groups of children supervised and cared for by young girls, aged women and those pregnant or just delivered? Neither the presence of a large number of Virginia-born slaves in the States to the South nor the number of mulattoes found throughout Virginia convicts the people of Virginia of sexual irregularities among, or with, their slaves for the purpose of increasing their human chattels. The negro needs little prompting towards procreation. The birth of very light skinned mulattoes has not become a thing unknown to this day.

U. B. Phillips in his *American Negro Slavery*, p. 361, declares that he has "but a single concrete item" to support the charge of deliberate breeding. That occurred in Massachusetts in the year 1636. The present writer has found but one other and that in Maryland. (Frederick Douglass, *Narrative of the Life of Frederick Douglass*, pp. 62, 63.)

[33] *Constitutional Whig*, March 28, 1832.

[34] *House Journal*, 1831-32, p. 109.

abolition of slavery in this commonwealth, have according to
order, had the same under consideration, and submit the following report and resolution.

Profoundly sensible of the great evils arising from the
condition of the colored population of this Commonwealth;
induced by humanity as well as policy to an immediate effort
for the removal in the first place as well of those who are now
free, as of such as may hereafter become free; believing that
this effort while it is in just accordance with the sentiments
of the community on the subject will absorb all our present
means; and that a further action for the removal of the slaves
should await a more definite development of public opinion,

Resolved as the opinion of this committee that it is inex-
pedient for the present to make any legislative enactments for
the abolition of slavery.[35]

With the suggestion of future action touching
slavery and the hope of removing the free negroes
before them, the delegates cast their votes for or
against this fateful report.[36] The final vote, 65-58,
gave slavery a new hold upon Virginia and the
South.[37]

[35] Ibid., p. 110. In the Journal the resolution is reported above on
the same page.

[36] Thomas Nelson Page (*The Old South,* p. 302) after describing
the treatment of Garrison by the Boston mob of 1835 says: "All of
this was within three years of the time when a bill to abolish slavery
in Virginia had failed in her General Assembly by only one vote."
As we see there never was such a bill submitted to the House, nor
is there a one-vote majority recorded for any vote during the close
of the debate.

[37] *House Journal,* 1831-32, p. 110.

CHAPTER V

Debate in the General Assembly on the Removal Bill

Scarcely had Virginia freed herself from the advances of State Emancipation and dismissed it from her House of Delegates, when she found Black Colonization pressing its suit with renewed vigor. Two days after the adoption of the report of the select committee on the colored population, Brodnax, for that committee, reported a bill to the end of colonizing the free negro on foreign shores.

While a large majority of the House was convinced that the free black was a menace to the peace of society and that his removal was a consummation devoutly to be wished, there arose a sharp division as to the means of securing colonists. Some would create a great system adequate to transport the free blacks to Liberia, with the expectation that applications for removals would tax the capacity of the system. Others, led by General Brodnax, were opposed to erecting this machinery and leaving its success dependent upon the disposition of the negroes. Nor was this their only objection to basing such a program upon the voluntary action of the people they sought to remove. Failure to provide legal coercion could but result in the employment of inhumane extra-legal methods in the course of converting free negroes to the idea of leaving this land in which they were united by strong ties with others of their race for one of which they knew little.

For the legislature to divide and quibble over the compulsory feature of the bill was stupid, if the speakers were sincere in their declarations. Had not the State already forbidden free negroes to remain longer than a year after manumission? Did not the act of April 1831 declare that such an offender should be liable to arrest and sale unless he were protected by a license from the General Assembly?[1] This being the fact, wherein lay the objection to providing a place of emigration and obliging the negroes to go there, all the while exercising far more care for their social and connubial ties than was possible under the existing laws? The legislators could hardly have been totally unaware of this statute, for in the preceding session wherein many of them sat, nine petitions for permission to remain were rejected, while before the present House similar petitions lay.

On Monday, January 30, the committee reported a resolution which was adopted without debate: " Resolved, That it is expedient to apply to the General Government to procure a territory or territories beyond the limits of the United States, to which the several states may remove their free colored population."[2] After its adoption, Brodnax became aware

---

[1] *Acts of The Assembly,* 1830-31, p. 107.
[2] *Constitutional Whig,* January 31, 1832.

of the fact that this was putting the cart before the horse, for if the House did not adopt a plan of colonization, application to the United States would be useless. He therefore demanded the reconsideration of the resolution, but this was denied by the House. Next day he moved the reference of the bill to the committee of the whole and that it be made the order of the day for February 6th. Witcher opposed vehemently, but to no avail. Carter of Prince William joined in urging that this question " only less important than the question which had already been discussed " [3] be considered by the whole house in committee assembled. It was so ordered.

It may be recalled that on December 12 Rives offered a resolution in regard to devoting to the removal of free negroes such money as Virginia should receive from the Federal Government. On February 1 the committee reported adversely declaring its opposition to the disposal of the funds in that manner.[4]

On Monday, February 6, the House, according to order, resolved itself into a committee of the whole and took up the removal bill. After the bill was read, Brodnax called attention to the first section. The fundamental principle upon which the whole structure was built was that the Central Board of Commissioners for the Removal of Free Persons of Color should be clothed with powers of coercion. If

[3] *Richmond Enquirer,* January 31, 1832.
[4] *House Journal,* 1831-32, p. 125.

this principle were retained, little amendment would
be required, but if rejected, general revision of the
whole bill would be necessary. Therefore to save
time, he asked that this feature be considered at once,
and the better to get it before the House he invited
some gentleman opposing coercion to move an
amendment to the first section. This section read:

Be it enacted by the General Assembly, That all persons of
colour within this commonwealth, who are now free, or who
may hereafter become free therein, shall, in the manner, in
the order, under the limitation, and with the exceptions,
herein after provided be removed from this State, to Liberia,
or such other place or places on the western coast of Africa,
as may be approved and designated by the Central Board of
Commissioners for the removal of free persons of colour,
herein after constituted; or to such other place or places
beyond the limits of the United States, as may by law be
designated; and after such removal shall be supported in
cases of individuals destitute of the means beyond an extent
herein after defined at the expense of the State, for such
reasonable periods of time and to such amounts as . . . .
specified.[5]

John C. Campbell complied with the request of
Mr. Brodnax and moved that " with their own consent " be inserted after " shall." [6]

Mr. Brodnax followed in defense of the compulsory
feature. To him the only question of real magnitude
was the fundamental one of the will of the legislature

[5] House Journal, 1831-32, App. Document No. 7, A Bill Providing
For the Removal of Free Persons of Colour From this Commonwealth.

[6] Constitutional Whig, February 9, 1832.

to send the free blacks out of Virginia. To determine
the proper procedure of giving effect to the affirmative answer of that question was easy. There was
but one proper way and that plain. The Board must
be empowered to execute its orders, the subject
willing or not. For gentlemen to profess themselves
in favor of removing the free blacks but opposed to
coercion was absurd. Belief that the negroes would
embrace the opportunity in large numbers was
founded in ignorance. But a few days before, he,
Brodnax, had inquired of a gentleman, with excellent
opportunities to judge, how many free blacks would
voluntarily leave Richmond. From him came the reply that not one would be willing to go. But even
if it were granted that a fourth, or even a third,
were willing, Brodnax would not burden the State
with so imperfect a remedy.

If legal coercion was denied there was a consequence of inevitable occurrence that filled him with
horror even in contemplation. He doubted not that
the capacity of the system would be constantly taxed
whether legal coercion was exercised or not. Though
removal were to be accomplished only with the consent of the subjects there would always be a large
waiting list. People would not only consent to go
but beg to be taken:

" But what sort of consent,—a consent extorted by a series
of oppressions calculated to render their situation among us
insupportable. . . . . Who does not know that when a free
negro, by crime or otherwise has rendered himself obnoxious

to a neighborhood, how easy it is for a party to visit him one
night, take him from his bed and family, and apply to him
the gentle admonition of a severe flagellation, to induce him
to consent to go away. In a few nights the dose can be
repeated, perhaps increased, until in the language of the
physician, quantum suff. has been administered to produce the
desired operation; and the fellow then becomes perfectly
willing to move away.[7]

That Brodnax was not the only one convinced
that forceful persuasion would be used if legal
coercion was denied, was attested when Fisher and
Chandler expressed themselves to the same effect.
Flagellation would be but one of the objectionable
consequences attendant upon the adoption of such
a scheme. Driven violently and suddenly from their
homes, the negroes would be able to save little of
what property they might own and find it almost
impossible to realize anything on crops then growing. Social and connubial ties would in many cases
be disrupted with great suffering. How much better,
how much more humane to have the emigrants col-
lected by a legal agency, acting under strict regulation, exercising a paternal care over their property, considering their family ties, and executing
the certain and inevitable will of the State in an
orderly manner.

Mr. Bryce of Goochland felt about coercion in the
same way as Mr. Campbell so far as it affected those
negroes permitted by law to remain in the State,
but saw no reason for protecting others from this

[7] *Richmond Enquirer,* February, 14, 1832.

feature of the bill. To this effect he offered an amendment, but it was quickly rejected. Campbell withdrew his amendment and moved, in substitute, to strike out the words " or who may hereafter become free therein " and to add after " shall," " with their own consent " making this part read: " That all persons of colour within this commonwealth who are now free, shall with their own consent, in the manner. . . . ." After debate this amendment was adopted by a vote of 66-42.[8]

An attempt of Morris to kill the bill by indefinite postponement failed 28-94.[9]

Mr. Gholson was confident that there could be no " constitutional impediment . . . . to the adoption of the compulsory principle," but he did not consider it indispensable to the successful execution of the enterprise. He challenged any one to show that either in Virginia or any other State free blacks were entitled to the immunities and privileges of citizens. Public opinion, he believed, afforded the Board an adequate lever. Public opinion was in favor of removal. Public opinion would be an irresistible agent in carrying out the provisions of the law. When the means of his removal was provided, the free black would be expelled by that mighty influence, and that without cruelty and injustice.

Gholson hazarded the opinion that for the next few years emigration would need little stimulation.

[8] *Constitutional Whig*, February 9, 1832.
[9] Ibid., February 9, 1832.

Was not the Colonization Society at the moment
unable to furnish means of conveyance for the numbers eager to go? If the State were but to provide
transports and permit manumission for the purpose,
masters would in increasing numbers rid themselves
of their slaves. The removal of all willing candidates
completed, it would be soon enough to have " public
opinion " express itself in firmer forms. By termi-
nating contracts, further limiting his personal liberty,
and generally restricting his ability to make a living
the State could expel the negro without flogging. By
some vagary of reasoning, Gholson attacked legal
coercion and unwittingly suggested in substitute
means equally harsh and cruel. He would have nothing to do with " direct legislative coercion or putting
them out because we had the power [but] would force
them out by restricting their means of making a
living." [10]

The question being taken upon the adoption of the
amendment of the committee of the whole, it was
passed by the House, 71-54.[11] The compulsory feature expunged from the bill, the latter was returned
to the colored population committee for drastic
revision.

On Saturday, February 11, Brodnax reported a
substitute bill having respect for the consent of the
free negroes.

The Central Board of Commissioners, tempo-
rarily composed of the Governor and the Council,

[10] *Richmond Enquirer,* February 24, 1832.
[11] *House Journal,* 1831-32, p. 136.

was granted large powers to maintain resident and itinerant agents, charter ships, contract for supplies, hire out negroes, borrow money, and generally execute the law. For greater clarity we quote the fifth section:

In effecting the removal of free persons of colour as aforesaid the appropriation for each year, shall be exclusively applied in the first instance, to the removal and subsequent temporary support . . . . of those free negroes and mulattoes who are entitled by existing laws of the state to remain in it, but who voluntarily consent to remove, and apply to the said central board or its agents. . . . . The next class which shall be preferred for deportation, after all the applicants of the former class at any time shall have been provided for, shall consist of such free persons of colour as may consent to be transported. When these shall in like manner be exhausted, the next class . . . . shall consist of those who may hereafter be manumitted for the purpose, but for whose removal, the former owner shall have made no provision. Those negroes and mulattoes who may hereafter be emancipated for the purpose and for whose removal and subsequent temporary support the former owner shall have provided sufficient means and those who not being entitled to remain in the State, but not consenting to remove shall have been hired out until a sufficient sum is raised to defray the expenses of their removal and subsequent support as aforesaid . . . . shall be removed by the Board as soon as they may find it practicable and convenient.[12]

Supplementary to the provision for hiring out the last group, the sixth section explained in detail the manner of letting them out. None were required to labor under the supervision of the sheriff and county

[12] *Senate Journal,* 1831-32, App. Bill No. 2, p. 2.

8

courts longer than two years. Any deficiency in
their wages the State should make up. No man or
woman above the ages of forty-five and forty years
respectively should be shipped except with his or
her consent or upon special order of the court. Connubial ties were protected by the clause forbidding
the separation of husbands and wives. Children
under the ages of sixteen and fourteen for males and
females respectively were not to be separated from
their parents. The Board was granted '' a sound
and humane discretion '' in arranging shipments.
For the comfort and support of the colonists upon
their arrival the Board was directed to provide
tools, clothing, shelter, food, and other requisites for
one year.[13]

The attack on appropriations was not long de-
layed. George Wilson moved to strike out the appropriation for 1833, $100,000, and substitute $50,-
000. On the suggestion of Archibald Bryce the
motion was divided. Debate on the first part ensued.
Archibald Bryce naïvely argued that the appropriation should be small so that the appropriation for
the following year might be the larger. Brodnax
ridiculed an appropriation of $50,000, and asked
that if the House were in earnest it grant $200,000.
He must have been more convinced than ever of the
insincerity of certain members, Gholson and Archibald Bryce especially, who, professing to be anxious
to accomplish the removal of the free negroes, were

[13] *Constitutional Whig,* February 18, 1832.

again found binding the arm of the Board. The appropriation was easily within the means of the State. In fact, John C. Campbell asserted that it could be readily met with the expected revenues without increasing taxation.[14]

If all the House had been of one mind with Miers W. Fisher of Northampton, Brodnax could have secured more than the appropriation he desired. A few days before, one of the gentlemen from Fauquier, probably Marshall, had argued that the State was without adequate means successfully to attempt colonization. Fisher replied with the argument that not only were the means at hand but that the removal could be readily effected and that to the pecuniary advantage of society. He would ask the gentleman from Fauquier if he had counted the cost of maintaining the free blacks. In Northampton, not half of them supported themselves but lived by their own theft and that of their friends and relatives in bondage. This condition was not peculiar to Northampton County but common to all. Assuming the same ratio, he found 25,000 blacks living on the profits of others. At the minimum rate of subsistence, six and a quarter cents *per diem,* they cost the Commonwealth $525,500 [15] annually. Plainly their removal at any figure less than that would be a profitable investment.[16]

[14] Ibid.
[15] More accurately $570,300.
[16] *Richmond Enquirer,* February 14, 1832.

But the majority of the House were decidedly of a different opinion. After Daniel concluded his speech in favor of reducing the appropriation, in the course of which he dragged in the trite argument " that the people had not expressed themselves," the House struck out the $100,000 by a vote of 53-51.[17]

Having purged the bill of this excessive sum, the House found itself debating one of $90,000. Preston, timorous because " the people had not expressed themselves," hoped gentlemen would be conservative and agree on $50,000. After debate by Brodnax, John C. Campbell, Bolling, Summers, the irrepressible Witcher, and Bryce, the greater sum was inserted in the blank. Truly $10,000 must have been an enormous sum for these worthy legislators.

J. Thompson Brown moved to amend the fifth section of the bill by which provision was made for the removal of " those who may hereafter be manumitted for the purpose, but for whose removal, the former owner shall have made no provision." The present program contemplated the extinction of the free black population with its normal increase in a short period of years. Not less than ten years would be required. Rather than have this population constantly augmented, Brown advised that the negroes be held subject to the firm rule of slavery until the State should be ready to remove them. If the existing law against manumission were unaltered and this provision removed from the bill, the failing ranks of the free

[17] *Constitutional Whig,* February 18, 1832.

blacks would be supplemented only by negroes whose
immediate transportation was assured. Without
doubt, the effect of this amendment would be to keep
the waiting list at a minimum. To that extent it was
of value, but upon the negro it would have brought
increased suffering. Social and family ties would be
the worse ruptured because of the inability of masters to free the friends and relatives of those about
to be transported.

Brown was supported by Gholson on this measure, but the right stout defender of the bill in its
fullest powers, Brodnax, aided by John C. Campbell
and Marshall, was able to preserve it unamended.
The friends of the bill scored their largest majority
in the rejection of this motion, 60-41.[18]

The attention of the House again settled on expenditures. The tenth section contained provision
for an annual appropriation of $200,000 after the
year 1833. A motion to amend by striking out this
section, first made by Marshall and renewed by Good,
of Berkeley, was sustained.[19] Not a few there were
who felt that, until success proved the wisdom of
their action, they did enough in binding the State for
the years 1832 and 1833. For the remainder of 1832
the Board was granted $35,000, a sum which the
chairman of the finance committee declared could
be supplied from the expected revenue.[20] For the
temporary shelter of the colonists $10,000 was set

[18] Ibid.
[19] Ibid.
[20] Ibid.

aside. Completing his labors along these lines, Marshall caused the House to strike out the clause defining the sum to be applied to equipping each immigrant with food and other essentials, leaving this matter to the discretion of the Commissioners. After allowing the Board discretion in locating the colony, the House ordered that the bill be engrossed.

The next day, February 16, the bill was taken up again, read the third time, and passed by a vote of 79-41.[21]

The Senate for the first time found itself confronted with the negro problem. There had been long debate in the House of Delegates upon the subject of emancipation. Petitions, letters to the press, editorials, resolutions of public meetings, prophecies of dire distress, and even threats to divide the State had played their part in influencing that body, but the Senate had passed these months in peace and quiet. The decision of the House not to undertake any scheme of abolition secured the Senate against the prodding or censure of the people on this delicate subject. The removal bill held the interest of the State upon that body three weeks longer, but now had come the moment when the Senate must play its part in the solution of the colored population problem which so troubled the State.

Unfortunately for those who would know more than the barest outline of what occurred or the number of votes cast for or against this or that measure,

[21] *House Journal,* 1831-32, p. 158.

who would know the reasons and influences that caused the Senate to reject this bill so pregnant with good, the local press upon which we have been forced to rely for a fuller account of the proceedings than that found in the journals, fails us at this point. Although carrying full accounts of proceedings and speeches in the House of Delegates, the local papers give exceedingly little information about the Senate that cannot be found in the journal. Happily, it is more complete than that of the House.

On February 17 the bill was taken up, read the first and second times, and on the motion of Mr. Dromgoole, chairman of the Committee of General Laws, laid on the table. After desultory attempts to amend and a motion by George Booker to postpone indefinitely, it was on March 6 seriously debated.

The fifth section of the bill divided the free colored population under the age limits into five classes in which order they were to be removed, that is: 1, those who, although allowed to dwell in the State, present themselves for transportation; 2, those who having no license to remain present themselves; 3, those who shall be emancipated for the purpose but whose emancipation should be unaccompanied by provision for their transportation; 4, those who should be emancipated with provision; and 5, those at the moment dwelling within the State contrary to law but indisposed to emigrate.

Upon the first class there was no division of opinion. The second was immediately attacked by George Booker with a motion to strike it from the list, but it weathered his attack with a majority of nine votes.[22] Dromgoole offered amendments in succession to strike out the third, fourth, and fifth classes together with the remainder of the section. The amendments were severally rejected, the first by a tie 15-15.[23] Four days later, however, he prevailed upon the Senate, the fourth rule of order to the contrary, to reconsider his amendment and the third class was stricken from the bill.[24]

The tenth section carrying appropriations was fiercely attacked. Booker moved the erasure of the whole, but in this he was unsuccessful. The appropriation for 1833 was reduced from $90,000 to $50,000. Francis E. Rives, Senator from Isle of Wight, Prince George, Sussex, Surry, and Southampton counties, perhaps oblivious of the late massacre, certainly untouched and uninstructed by its horrors, moved the omission of even this sum.

The sixth section was largely concerned with the removal of negroes unlawfully residing in the State and unwilling to emigrate. Patteson protested against the course proposed, hiring them out by order of court. No, burden not the State with such willful offenders. If they refuse to emigrate, let them

---

[22] *Senate Journal,* 1831-32, p. 149.
[23] Ibid., p. 148.
[24] Ibid., p. 166.

be taken up and sold by the sheriff in conformity with the act of April 7, 1831. To that end he moved the erasure of the major part of the section and the insertion of a sentence subjecting them to the aforesaid act.[25]

Two months earlier western members of the House of Delegates, during the slavery debate, were calling loudly upon their eastern brothers to think not of the pecuniary interests of their constituents, but in a lofty, loyal devotion to Virginia to sacrifice these considerations to the good of the Commonwealth. Lest the East think the West presumptuous and officious because of its active participation in this debate, the latter pleaded the common and indivisible interest of the Commonwealth. True the West had few slaves but in this good State the ruin of one section was the ruin of the other, the prosperity of one the blessing of the other. But with the relative pecuniary interests reversed, the voice from beyond the mountains was less loud in its declamation of the indivisible nature of the weal or woe of the State. Having some 6,000 free negroes, or about an eighth of the 47,000 in Virginia, the West, were the bill passed unamended, would be called on for a fraction of the appropriation in excess of her fraction of the affected population. In this light the pecuniary interest of the tax payers beyond the mountains loomed large, and devotion to the State, while an excellent thing in the abstract or when

[25] Ibid., p. 155.

urged upon others, was seen to be good for home
consumption only when exercised within reason.

This sentiment, that the West should not be
loaded with the burdens of the East but be taxed
only for local expenditures, found expression in the
mouth of Charles Morgan, Senator from Preston,
Monongalia, and Randolph counties. In lieu of the
first half of the bill, Morgan offered a substitute of
six sections removing the essential control and responsibility from the State and fastening them upon
the county and local corporation. The tone of the
substitute is clearly sounded in the first section:

> Be it enacted by the General Assembly of Virginia, That
> such of the free negroes and mulattoes in this Commonwealth,
> desiring to remove beyond the limits of the United States, as
> the courts of the counties and corporations respectively within
> which they may reside, shall think proper to provide for,
> shall be removed to such place or places, as the Governor
> shall designate, and be supported after their removal, for
> a reasonable time, at the expense of the counties and corpora-
> tions, respectively from whence they shall have been so
> removed.[26]

The third section authorized the Auditor and
Treasurer to keep separate books " so as to exhibit
at all times the exact amount of money received to
the credit of each county and corporation and also
the amount disbursed for the transportation of free
negroes and mulattoes therefrom." The antagonism
of Eastern counties was of course aroused by this

[26] Ibid., p. 167.

attempt to shift the burden. Strange to relate Morgan's substitute failed for want of two votes.[27]

Despite the vehement demand that "Something must be done" lest the deaths in Southampton should be entirely barren, despite the widespread and heated debate at hustings, fireside, and ordinary, despite the fact that the abolition struggle had proved abortive, despite the stern fear that dictated the adoption of a drastic police bill and the reformation of the militia, the Senate listened with favor to John G. Joynes, who, in the language of the Senate journal, "moved to postpone further consideration of the said bill indefinitely, and on the question being put thereon, it was agreed to by the Senate. Ayes 18, Noes, 14."[28]

Among the petitions presented to the General Assembly looking to the removal of free negroes that from Northampton was distinguished by its primary objective and consequent success in the halls of legislation. In this county, washed on the one side by the Atlantic Ocean and on the other by the Chesapeake Bay, dwelled three thousand five hundred and seventy-three whites with their three thousand seven hundred and thirty-four slaves and thirteen hundred and thirty-four free negroes. Behind it lay the small county of Accomac and farther still

---

[27] Ibid., p. 169.

[28] Ibid., p. 169. Beverly B. Munford (*Virginia's Attitude Toward Slavery and Secession*, p. 47) declares that " This bill so fraught with far-reaching consequences, was subsequently defeated in the Senate by one vote." The *Senate Journal* nowhere confirms this statement.

Maryland. At the nearest point, the mainland of Virginia, lay some ten miles away.

To the uneasiness common to counties having a negro population larger than the white, was added, in the case of Northampton, fear born of isolation. In the late massacre dispatches had been sent rapidly overland in all directions and troops converging from distant parts found no large bodies of water impeding their march. Forgetting the rapid transport of troops down the James to Smithfield, the people of Northampton apprehended greater difficulty in suppressing insurrection because of the delays of water transport. While the Bay might permit of rapid relief in fair weather, in time of storm or in the event that messengers were unable to leave the peninsula, it would completely cut off that county.

Seriously alarmed, the people of Northampton met in public meeting to improve their ability to resist and quell insurrectionary movements among their slaves. While not likely to join the first bands, the free blacks were potential allies of their brothers of color. Their removal was therefore eminently desirable. Imperative as seemed the necessity of removing them, the citizens of Northampton refused to expel them only to infest other sections of the State, but undertook their removal to Liberia. Their petition differed essentially from others in that its primary object was authority to act upon their own resources. Following a lengthy preamble setting forth the situation of the county and their apprehensions, the citizens adopted a series of thoroughgoing and interesting resolutions:

5. That to effect their [the negroes] removal John Eyre . . . . [and others] be a committee to borrow a sum of money not exceeding fifteen thousand dollars; for the payment of which a tax shall annually be imposed upon each citizen of this county equal to the tax he may pay to the state; so that such tax be at least equal to his revenue tax of the present year, until the principle [sic] and interest shall be paid. . . . .

10. That after the arrangements for their removal have been made we pledge ourselves not to employ or have any dealing whatever with any free negro in the county.

11. That we pledge ourselves not to rent to any free negro any house or land, and that we will forthwith give notice to those with whom we have contracted to quit on the first day of June next.

12. That we earnestly recommend to the owners of vessels in the county, immediately or as soon as practicable, to discontinue the use and employment of slaves, and free negroes on board their vessels; as we do firmly believe the practice dangerous to the peace & safety of our society.[29]

In addition to requiring her representatives in the legislature to secure a bill giving effect to these resolutions, Northampton directed them to vote for every " measure whether of a general or local character which may have for its object the removal of the free people of colour from the State or any part thereof." Upon receipt of an act empowering them

[29] *Petitions to the General Assembly,* 1831, Northampton, December 6.

to act, John Eyre and his committee were to ac-
quaint the free negroes with their purpose and enter
into correspondence with the Colonization Society.
The signatures of one hundred and ninety-six people followed the resolutions.

While the sum of $15,000 seems small to us accus-
tomed to appropriations in millions, Northampton
was taking a bold step. Neglecting costs of adminis-
tration, this sum would suffice for the transportation
of four hundred and sixteen negroes, thirty-one per
cent. of that class. Assuming that other factors remained unchanged, it would be another generation
before this loss was made good, during which time
the whites would have so outdistanced the blacks,
that though the absolute strength of the latter might
be recruited, it would be relatively weaker. If the
body of émigrés were well chosen to include only the
young and vigorous, the blow would be multiplied
in its effect. If the tax for the funding of the debt
were kept equal to that paid to the State for the
current year, nine years would more than suffice to
erase the debt if no account were taken of interest.
For the current year just closing, Northampton
paid on carriages, slaves, gigs, coaches, and land
$1857.62.[30] A second application of this sovereign
remedy at the end of a decade would be productive
of marked results.

Scarcely was the Governor's Message read and a
committee appointed to deal with the colored popu-

[30] *House Journal,* 1831-32. Appendix Document 2 C.

lation when Miers W. Fisher of Northampton, with
dispatch commensurate with the zeal of his constituents, presented their petition and the House referred
it to the committee. This petition distinguished in
priority was no less conspicuous in its fruition in
appropriate legislation.

Immured in the committee, months passed ere the
petition gained the attention of the House on February 16, at which time Brodnax reported a bill in conformity with the wishes of the petitioners. The
House, more interested in the police bill, considered
in the next chapter, and absorbed in the removal
bill passed this day, postponed consideration of the
Northampton bill. On the 25th it was again before
the House long enough to be ordered engrossed.
Long debate on the removal bill had exhausted the
arguments for and against African Colonization,
hence little interest accompanied the progress of this
bill. Affecting them in no manner, those who had so
loudly declaimed against removal on a state-wide
basis forgot, or overlooked, the horrors and evils
which prevented their voting in favor of the first
scheme of removal. So apathetic was the House that
the bill was engrossed and read " by general
consent " and passed amid a pervading lack of
interest.[31]

Passage in the Senate was equally rapid and un-
interesting. It was immediately entrusted to a committee headed by John G. Joynes. The next day

[31] Ibid., p. 189.

slightly modified, it was reported to the whole body. Three days thereafter it passed.

The most ardent among the signers of the petition could scarcely have been disappointed in the plenary investment of authority conferred upon the committees. '' Be it therefore enacted, That the proceedings of the said public meetings and the acts done or to be done by the said committee in pursuance of the authority vested in them as aforesaid shall be, and the same are hereby declared to be valid and obligatory, so far as the same may not violate or contravene any law of this commonwealth.'' [32] All money that the committee might borrow in accordance with the resolutions should be chargeable to the county as any other debt incurred by agents of that county.[33]

[32] *Acts of the Assembly,* 1831-32, p. 23.

[33] In the annual reports of the American Colonization Society for the next three years there is no item suggesting a shipment of any considerable body of negroes from Northampton County.

CHAPTER VI

Repression

If the attempts to abolish slavery and colonize the free black be considered direct consequences of the Southampton Insurrection, petitions from Petersburg, Charles City, New Kent, Buckingham, and Culpeper counties may be deemed indirect or secondary effects. Not that the conditions of which they complained arose suddenly, but in the widespread will to treat the negro problem the petitioners found stimulus and support. These petitions were nourished by the disturbed condition of the public mind.

The progressive invasion of their trade by negroes, free and slave, produced in the breasts of white mechanics a spirit of antagonism and drove the more bold to settle their affairs and join the steady stream of emigrants coursing down the western side of the mountains. An " unprecedented migration of the labouring classes " [1] during the fall of 1831 disturbed the landowners of Culpeper. Taught by abolitionists and removalists, they prayed the interposition of the legislature.

Though slaveholders, in some instances owners of " mechanic slaves," they advised the passage of a law prohibiting the apprenticing of negroes to learn

---

[1] *MS. Petitions to the Legislature,* 1831, Culpeper, December 9.

trades. Let penalties fall upon both the masters of
apprenticed negroes and their instructors. Already
the trades of mason, plasterer, smith, painter, shoe-
maker, miller, and distiller were largely practiced
by blacks, degrading these trades and throwing out
of work white labor. Unable to support themselves
and families, too proud to compete with slaves,
white mechanics fled from the country in numbers
unparalleled in the preceding ten years. A correc-
tive was imperiously required, for Virginia could
ill afford this drain upon her manhood.

The prayer from Culpeper was echoed two days
later, December 11, by the petition of two hundred
and twenty-six mechanics of Petersburg. They, the
victims, of the black invasion, asked specific and
immediate remedy. After assuring the Assembly
that they did not fear wholesome competition of a
uniform and systematic character competent to
" secure the public from exaction,"[2] but only that
with irresponsible negroes, the mechanics enlisted in
their favor the general excitement prevalent throughout the State by calling attention to the dangers
attendant upon this system of itinerant slave
mechanics. Of what use would be statutes limiting
the right of slaves to move about if blacksmiths were
allowed to journey from place to place in the per-
formance of their master's business? Unwatched by
master, or overseer, they were doubly capable of

[2] MS. *Petitions to the General Assembly,* 1831, Dinwiddie, December 11.

mischief. To the facility they enjoyed of becoming channels of " communications for evil purposes " must be added the opportunity of " fabricating the very instruments of mischief " and distributing them to their brothers of color.

In remedy the mechanics asked restrictive regulation of their black competitors. Require that in every shop operated by a slave the master maintain a white overseer constantly employed in the same trade. Prevent slaves " going at large " except for the commission of specific tasks arranged beforehand by the master himself. Let all payments for such work be made to the master in person. Punish employers hiring under other conditions with heavy fines.

From Charles City and New Kent counties came a joint protest against the employment of negroes as millers. By them the good people of these counties were subjected to " numerous cheateries and deceptions " by virtue of which squads of free negroes loafing around the mills were kept alive. It was enough to suffer the loss of grain, but to support squads of free negroes " by which we believe much injury is done to our best interest " was unbearable. The mills themselves were veritable hot-beds of sedition in which drivers with grain were exposed to infection.[3]

[3] MS. Petitions to the General Assembly, 1831, Charles City, December 27.

One phase of the relation of master and slave presented a tangle of infinite difficulty. This form of property the master could use to great evil with but little or no danger to his purse or person. Did a neighbor anger him, how easy to drive a slave to burn his stable! Little the slave's testimony would avail against the master's denial. Did his neighbor have large stores of meat and well-filled granaries while his own yawned in their emptiness? His slave could bring home the bacon. If caught, thirty-nine lashes upon his black back pained his master not at all. Civil suit was futile did the master disclaim complicity in the crime. The enormity of this condition was strikingly revealed by comparing the liability of owners of different kinds of property. If a bull broke out and killed a slave the master of the slave could sue. But if the reverse were true, if the slave killed the bull, the owner of the bull had but the scant satisfaction of seeing " thirty-nine lashes well laid on " applied to the dusky toreador. Owners of fierce dogs might be required to keep them up, but owners of slaves could not be compelled to give security for their good behavior however vicious they might be. Even for slaves executed for murder the master received compensation.

In the Auditor's Report for 1831 is listed the item of $15,000 paid for slaves condemned to transportation or death. The affair with Nat is reflected in the

sum of $9,400 spent since the first of October.[4] This
compensation was not a total loss, for the sale of
" transports " yielded a considerable sum. In the
same report the revenue from this source for the
year is estimated to be $10,000,[5] largely based on
the expected sale of twenty-eight convicts then on
hand.[6]

That the master should not be responsible for his
slave but should receive compensation from the State
in the event that it took precaution to prevent the
repetition of his crime, aroused the protest of Washington and Buckingham counties.

In the former two decisions given by the local
court required the masters involved to give security
for the good behavior of their slaves. In lieu of this
security, the slaves concerned were incarcerated, but
were subsequently released by the Superior Court
which declared that a " slave could not be held to
security for his good behavior or . . . . his master
for him." [7] The petitioners very pertinently ask, if
that be the law " Why should a slave be the only
lawless human being in the community? If the

---

[4] The Assembly received five petitions on the part of persons who
had lost eight slaves in the suppression of the Insurrection, praying
that they might receive the value of their negroes. More justifiable
was the petition for compensation for a slave killed while actually in
arms in defense of Dr. Blunt's house. *MSS. Petitions to the General Assembly,* 1831, Southampton.

[5] *House Journal,* 1831-32, Appendix Document No. 2, pp. 14-16.

[6] MS. April 11, 1832, the Auditor received from James Goodwin
$10,745 for 34 convicts. (*Executive Papers,* 1832, March 1-May 31.)

[7] *MS. Petitions to the Legislature,* 1831, Washington, Dec. 17.

master is unwilling to be bound for him, he must be dangerous and ought to be sent out of the country."[8] The citizens of Buckingham also demanded that masters be responsible for damages and thefts committed by their slaves and that the State be no longer required to pay for convicted slaves.

Master and slave taken care of, Fauquier produced a demand that free negroes, if not exiled, be required to give security that they would be of good behavior.[9]

In so far as particular acts were the object of these petitions they fell short of the mark. In the charge of the committees for Courts of Justice and the coloured population, the end came quietly. Brodnax was soon able to report their demise, and they were buried unwept and unsung. But on the police bill their influence was unmistakably impressed.

Endowed with a living superstition inherited from the Dark Continent, the negroes accorded their preachers a peculiar and exalted place. The plantation system contributed not a little to establish the black exhorter. Long toil and poor facilities to improve their mental state operated as narcotics upon the already listless disposition of the negro to make him a patient listener rather than a thinker or active debater. On Sunday few means of diversion,—hunting, fishing, gambling, and dancing,—bid against religion for attention. What a treat then to

[8] MS. Petitions to the Legislature, 1831, Buckingham, Dec. 16.

[9] MS. Petitions to the Legislature, 1832, Fauquier, February 2.

sing the melodies they loved, listen to the stories of that " better day acoming," and learn the latest gossip of friends and relatives on other plantations. Could he add a little smattering of learning to his talents, the negro preacher was a prophet in Israel.

With the pollution of this fountain of knowledge by missionaries of hate and insurrection, Virginia was attacked in a most serious fashion. Given incendiary tracts and pictures, misguided by abolitionists, enjoying a favored position in his society, the black preacher was capable of the greatest mischief.

" Veritas " writing to the local press expressed the sentiments of not a few when he advised against tolerating religious meetings conducted by black preachers or irresponsible whites:

To this I should not object, were it not perverted to unchristian, if not anti-christian, purposes, to the encouragement of discontent, insubordination and insurrection among the slaves and by consequence to bring confusion and wild disorder into families and civil society. The abstractions and general principles of Christianity are inculcated in slaves, in a language which they little understand, and to which the teacher himself in all probability, attaches no definite meaning. But the duties which Christianity commands and enjoins, as appropriate to their estate, are seldom or never mentioned; or if they be, are mentioned in a way so slightingly as to induce one to think that in the preacher's estimation, what is written to enforce positive duties and Christian morals are of so little worth, that it might as well be expunged from the sacred volume. Instead of these duties being taught and enjoined, the slaves are informed that God is no respecter of persons . . . . and that they are free in Christ—ergo that they ought to be absolutely free. . . . . Insubordination and its horrid consequences is the natural result of all they inculcate.[10]

As we have seen, Governor Floyd in his Message advised the quieting of the negro preacher and the revision of " all the laws intended to preserve in due subordination the slave population of our State." In this field of legislation the East and West found ground for common action: Halifax with its many slaves could join Harrison with its few; William O. Goode could count as his friend and coadjutor Samuel Moore. Revision of the police laws, not conferring benefits upon one section and burdens on the other but guarding the welfare of the whole, was a simple and easy process.

In the midst of the later stages of debate on the removal bill, Gholson reported the revised police bill. The House, otherwise engaged, paid but little attention to the newcomer. On the twenty-seventh of February, the committee again presented their bill. Before it could be withdrawn it had suffered major alterations.

The police bill was a *potpourri* of rare composition. In its nineteen sections were the strangest of ingredients from farm products to musical companies and bootlegged liquor. To licenses, larceny, assaults, riots, and insurrections, negro preachers and a dash of religious meetings gave peculiar, if not delicate, flavor. For seasoning chef Gholson

[10] *Richmond Enquirer,* September 2, 1831.

added " thirty-nine lashes well laid on." In preparation for so delectable a dish, Gholson contemplated a course of removal, but in this his plan went awry. Only on that basis can one account for the severity it embodied. On January 12 he spoke of expelling the free black with an economic lever. In this bill we see the fruition of that thought. So far as free negroes are concerned it is largely summed up in one sentence:

No free negro or mulatto, tradesman or mechanic shall after an opportunity has been presented to him on public means, or means other than his own, of removing from the State of Virginia to Liberia, or any other place without the limits of the United States, at which free persons of colour from Virginia may be colonized, be permitted to work at, or carry on his trade, or handicraft, in this Commonwealth, except by special permission of the court of the county or corporation in which he may reside. . . . .[11]

The sable preacher was accorded first place in this act, but not such a one as he would have chosen. With one stroke the House unfrocked him, forbidding him to preach or exhort by day or night. Did he forget, magistrates were authorized to remind him with as many lashes as his religious mind thinking on higher things might require. From Dr. Gholson's prescription it would seem that few were afflicted with more than thirty-nine-lash-power minds. For those suffering from chronic forgetfulness, a sea voyage in the care of a slave dealer was advised.

[11] *Senate Journal*, 1831-32, App. Bill No. 6, p. 3.

The laity was strictly enjoined not to tempt their divines by their presence. Only with passes from their masters, or in attendance upon them, were slaves permitted to go to night meetings even though conducted by whites. Attendance upon day meetings or gatherings of negroes on their own plantations were not forbidden. Masters might themselves, or through agents, instruct their slaves along religious lines.

The fourth section, restricting the right of free blacks to sell farm products or stock, was widely censured in the legislature and in the press. For the sale of such articles, even to a half dozen eggs, the vendor was required to present a certificate from a freeholder designating the articles, and declaring as his belief that the negro had acquired possession of them by honest means.

The sixth section we partially quoted. Only upon amendment by Brodnax were free negroes permitted to teach their own children trades. Colored barbers alone were allowed to take apprentices other than their sons. Carter's motion to strike out the ban forbidding negroes to join musical companies aroused the active opposition of Roane, Gholson, and Brodnax who feared that they would in this manner learn more of the art of war.

That they should possess or keep firearms of any kind whatsoever was intolerable. All persons dealing with slaves without permission of their owners were liable for losses the latter might suffer thereby.

The sale of spirituous liquors to slaves except under special permission, and disposal of liquors in any fashion by negroes within a mile of a muster or public meeting of any nature, were prohibited, the former under penalty of one hundred dollars.

The seventh section concerned seditious publications. It read as follows:

> If any person shall hereafter write, print, or cause to be written or printed any book, pamphlet, or other writing, advising persons of colour within this state to make insurrection, or to rebel, or shall knowingly circulate, or cause to be circulated, any book, pamphlet, or other writing, written or printed advising persons of colour in this commonwealth to commit insurrection; such person if a slave, free negro, or mulatto, shall on conviction before any justice of the peace be punished for the first offence with stripes . . . . and for the second offence, shall be deemed guilty of felony, and on due conviction shall be punished with death without benefit of clergy; and if the person so offending be a white person he or she shall be punished on conviction in a sum not less than one hundred nor more than one thousand dollars.[12]

The rigor of the bill worked not a little against it, though none of its provisions were worse than the old penalty for remaining in the State,—slavery. Of course, with the failure of the removal bill, it was excessive, but the police measure was passed in the House before the Senate postponed the other. An article in the *Virginia Advocate,* written while the colonization bill was yet before the Senate, probably expressed the sentiment of quite a large num-

[12] *Acts of the Assembly,* 1831, pp. 21, 22.

ber on the wisdom of mellowing the bill by the removal of its most severe features:

The Legislature has passed a law, which has for its object the removal of the free coloured population of Virginia from the limits of the State. Coercion is, however, not to be resorted to. The Legislature very wisely and humanely refused to make Force a part of their system. They seem willing however, to effect the same end though by different and we think more exceptionable means. We allude to that feature in the Police Bill . . . . which denies to those free negroes who refuse to avail themselves of the means offered by the State for emigrating to Liberia, the privilege of exercising any trade or handicraft whatever. One can hardly believe it possible that such a bill has in reality received the sanction of any body of men so respectable and intelligent as the Virginia Legislature. Yet such is the fact. Is this mercy to the free negro? Is it clemency in the State to say to him "we will not force you to go to Liberia, but you shall not live here"? It is in our estimation . . . . infinitely more odious, than open and avowed compulsion. It is cruel and barbarous in the last degree. Nor is it less cruel and unjust towards society generally than towards those who are more immediately the victims. There are thousands who will not go. . . . . They will stay and they must live. If the Legislature will not permit them to do so honestly they will do it as best they can. No law could be more admirably contrived to lend a helping hand to vice and crime. . . . . It is surely not difficult to conceive what will be the bad effect of this measure on our slave population and what facilities that population will afford the other class for living in Virginia despite of the Legislature and yet literally and strictly complying with its injunctions.[13]

[13] *Virginia Advocate in Constitutional Whig*, March 13, 1832.

Weathering two attempts to postpone it indefinitely, the bill was finally engrossed. In a final attempt to obstruct its passage John Chandler demanded reconsideration of the engrossing vote, but
the signal defeat of his motion, 38-89,[14] attests the
humor of the House. The question being put on
its passage it was adopted, 74-48,[15] and sent to the
Senate.

On Monday, March 5, the Senate, spurred on by
Dromgoole, relegated the bill to the tender mercies
of his Committee. A week later it emerged with
minor amendments. Booker moved to insert a long
section empowering local courts to require of free
negroes of bad fame security for their good behavior
under pain of transportation. If this became necessary, the victims should be hired out under supervision of the sheriff until he should have earned
enough to defray transportation charges to Liberia.[16]
Objection was wisely raised that dumping the refuse
of society upon the infant colony would work greatly
to its detriment. If these persons were intolerable
in a society long established and secure, how much
greater scourge would they be to a young settlement
yet struggling for existence.

The Senate purged the bill of its most cruel features. The fourth and seventh sections concerning
the sale of goods by free negroes and slaves were

[14] *House Journal*, 1831-32, p. 200.
[15] Ibid., p. 200.
[16] *Senate Journal*, 1831-32, p. 175.

removed. The prohibition on free negro mechanics
to practice their trade was denied and the ninth and
fourteenth sections meting out punishment to those
engaged in illicit traffic with slaves were likewise
stricken out.

On March 12 the bill was passed 19-10.[17] The next
day the House received the bill, but late in the year,
pressed by the rush of business, and perhaps discouraged by the defeat of the removal bill, there was
little heart for protracted debate. What were a few
amendments anyway when one recalled the abortive
attempt to abolish slavery and the inglorious efforts
to unburden the State of the free negro? Better the
bill with amendments than no bill at all. On the
motion of Randolph it was laid on the table.

On the fifteenth, on the motion of the same gentleman, it was taken up. Spurlock moved to postpone indefinitely this sole achievement of so much
work. Brodnax and Sims prevailed upon him to
withdraw his motion. The amendments severally
read were adopted and the bill passed, 74-78.[18]

[17] Ibid., p. 177.
[18] *House Journal*, 1831-32, p. 235.

CONCLUSION

The debate in the House of Delegates to abolish slavery proved disastrous to the cause of abolition in Virginia. The struggle was precipitated before its time. Anti-slavery sentiment had not reached proportions equal to carrying such a momentous program. The defeat was irreparable, for the discouraged liberals fell away, and a strong reaction set in. Many who had followed the debate with hope gave up the struggle, feeling that in truth there was no remedy less malignant than the disease they would cure. Never again in Virginia was the feeling against slavery so general, or the desire to see it abolished so strong. In the language of one just taking up his civic duties, " That was the culminating point—the flood tide of anti-slavery feeling which had been gradually rising for more than a century." [1]

From decrying slavery the sons of Virginia turned to its defence. In the measure that Northern abolitionists forsook denunciations of the slave system for appeals to the passions of the negroes and calumniations of their masters, the people of Virginia were driven to the defence of the institution. A philosophy exculpating masters was not long in developing. On January 30, but five days after the decision of the House not to undertake any action touching abolition, a memorial was presented from

[1] Philip Slaughter, *A Virginian History of African Colonization*, p. 55.

133

Hanover severely censuring the Assembly. In their
peroration the citizens of this county declared: [2]

We might have expected some law punishing with severity
the authors of incendiary publications. These publications
have proceeded from your own body. Your time might have
been usefully employed in reforming the police, in arming
the militia and providing for the public safety. It has been
worse than wasted in debating schemes which have rendered
property insecure, impaired the credit of the State, retarded
the improvement of your country, interrupted the domestic
relations of life, and brought disquiet and danger to our
firesides.

We therefore urge you as you regard the welfare of the
State to abstain from every attempt to provide for the emancipation of our slaves partial or general, immediate or prospec-
tive, in any manner whatsoever, and to adopt such a rule or
pass such an act as in future will assure the people that should
this delicate subject be again approached it shall be in secret
session, and above all to terminate your debates and return
to your constituents as speedily as possible.

A week later the *Enquirer* published a very critical
review of the debate under the title " The Letter of
Appomattox to the People of Virginia." It was soon
agreed that " Appomattox " was none other than
Benjamin Watkins Leigh. He was hardly more con-
siderate of the *amour propre* of the delegates than
were the memorialists of Hanover. He denied that
the dozen or more petitions before the House, with
their 1,188 signatures, represented the will of the
State or constituted sufficient authorization for the
course the House had pursued. But in common with

the petitioners, Leigh thought " something must be done." Since the State was utterly unable to extinguish slavery, reason dictated the adoption of means calculated to preserve the slaves in proper subordination. Three lines of action combined to promise undisturbed peace. First, let the militia be reformed, the citizenry armed, and the greatest vigilance maintained. Second, the election of proper persons to the Assembly would prevent the recurrence of debates similar to the last. Third, let the press be compelled to refrain from the advocacy of wild and fantastic schemes by the withdrawal of patronage from papers that might persist in that iniquitous practice.

Among the arguments adduced throughout the South in defence of slavery Dew's review of the debate in the Assembly stood out prominently.

Thomas Roderick Dew was born in King and Queen County December 5, 1802. A great part of his life was spent in Williamsburg, for after student days there he returned in 1827 to take the chair of history, metaphysics, and political economy in the College of William and Mary. Nine years later he was elected president, an office which he continued to fill until his death in 1846. His chief publications were *A Digest of the Laws, Customs, Manners, and Institutions of Ancient and Modern Nations* (1853), and the *Review of the Debate in the Virginia Legislature of 1831 and 1832*. The latter was widely read and was republished, under different titles, in 1849, 1852, and 1853.

10

In the edition of 1832 [3] the Review is a small book of but one hundred and thirty-three pages. Unlike the vast majority of his brothers-in-arms, if militant pens may justify the term, Dew did not base his work on the will of God or the Scriptures but depended upon economic and social arguments. The book falls readily into three logical divisions: slavery in the abstract, slavery in the United States, and the dangers and evils of slavery.

The origins of slavery were fourfold: war, disorder in civilized states, bargain and sale, and crime. Only as savages found that they could live by the labor of their captives did the practice of slaughtering them give place to that of making them slaves. In times of great disturbance and disorder the weak were glad to commit themselves into the hands of one mighty and able to protect them. Be the name as it may, to Dew it was in effect slavery. In periods of starvation men were eager to sell themselves that they might eat and not die of hunger. Could any object to slavery as a substitute for death in the punishment of crime? It was indisputable that slavery was not founded in injustice but in the amelioration of the severities of life.

Its contributions to civilization were large:

Slavery fells the forest, ... it gives rise to agricultural production, and thereby renders mankind less dependent on

[3] It had appeared earlier in a current periodical but was so abridged and mutilated that he published it separately. It is to the second edition of 1832 that reference will be made.

CONCLUSION 137

the precarious and diminishing production of the chase; it
thus gradually destroys the roving and unquiet life of the
savage; it furnishes a home and binds him down to the soil;
it converts the idler and wanderer into the man of business
and the agriculturist.[4]

Woman's exalted place in modern society was not
a little due to slavery. Not until captives worked
under the will of masters did the latter release their
women from the drudgery of the pastoral community. Her leisure and opportunities woman owed
to the chains of slaves beneath her. Only when their
chains were riveted did she cease to be a beast of
burden.

Quite properly slavery in the United States takes
up the major part of the book. Dew was of course
particularly concerned with Virginia. After relat-
ing the efforts of his native State to abolish the slave
trade and the difficulties she encountered with the
kings of England, he considered the plans of aboli-
tions and colonization proposed in the legislature.

The slaves in Virginia were worth not less than
$100,000,000.[5] The assessed value of lands and
houses for 1830 was $206,000,000. Removal and
colonization at $30 apiece would cost not less than
$14,000,000. Obviously the State could not purchase
the slaves and remove them at one stroke. Consider
then the possibility of removing the annual increase.
This would entail an annual charge on the treasury
of $1,380,000.

[4] Dew, p. 29.
[5] Ibid., p. 48.

But the problem was not so simple as that. Virginia lost about 6,000 negroes annually by sale or removal to the cotton States. If she were to enter the market for the purchase of this number of negroes, prices would rise and private buyers would be discouraged, thus lessening the ordinary drain. At the least, one could predict that the cost of purchasing the negroes to be removed would be increased.

Colonization would be impossible even if it were possible to remove the negroes from Virginia. Reports from Liberia proved the colony at best but a partial success. Shipments made by the Colonization Society taxed the expansive powers of the colony to the uttermost. The addition of six or seven thousand colonists annually would completely demoralize life there. The character and condition of the negro prevented his successful colonization. Only under the constant direction of white agents of the Society had Liberia been able to preserve itself. The climate was unsuited to the native of America, albeit of sable hue. The natives of districts contiguous to the settlement would keep up incessant warfare to prevent the occupation of their lands by Afro-Americans.

As it was impossible to colonize the negroes Dew feared some plan of abolition without colonization might be adopted:

We candidly confess, that we look upon this last mentioned scheme as much more practicable and likely to be forced upon us than the former. We consider it at the same time so fraught with danger and mischief both to the white and blacks—so utterly subversive of the welfare of the slave-holding country, in both an economical and moral point of view, that we cannot, upon any principle of right or expediency give it our sanction.[6]

There was little cause for perturbation. The negroes did not constitute at the moment a serious menace to the commonwealth. The future was fair. When the blacks and whites should have doubled, the danger from the former would not only have failed to hold its own but would have actually diminished. If the patrols were kept at the same ratio to the white population, they too would have doubled, but their effectiveness in ferreting out and quelling insubordination would have more than doubled. Even the figures presented in the Hanover memorial, Dew declared, argued for peace and order. Instead of an overwhelming preponderance of blacks, they presaged a gain by the whites. Little study was needed to show that the largest gain of the blacks had been made in the first decade of the nineteenth century and that since that period the percentage of increase had steadily diminished for the blacks and increased for the whites. In the decade just closed the whites east of the Blue Ridge Mountains multiplied at the rate of nearly eight per cent and the blacks at nine. For the entire State the rates were respectively fifteen and eleven per cent.[7]

[6] Ibid., p. 87.
[7] Ibid., p. 122.

Dew did not close his work without presenting a
remedy for the ills of his time. Emigration to the
Western States could not be stopped. That would
continue until the country should be saturated, but
extensive internal improvements would do much to
lessen this drain. Canals and railroads would cause
the flower of prosperity to burst into bloom both beyond the mountains and in the lowlands. In the
western counties agriculture, stimulated by cheaper
portage, would fill the pockets of the thrifty yeomanry and dispel thoughts of emigration. In the
lowlands cities would spring up and draw free white
labor from the North. Thus could Virginia not only
conserve, but augment her strength. The future lay
in building up a great white laboring class. In con-
nection with this labor, Dew made a startling con-
fession for so great a champion of slavery: '' We
believe that Virginia and Maryland are too far north
for slave labor, but all the states to the south of
these are perhaps better adapted to slave labor than
free.'' [8]

Dew developed his whole argument on the fundamental principle, security of property. If this were
granted, his conclusions were irrefutable. All would
admit that Virginia could not purchase the 470,000
slaves within her borders. If then she could not
confiscate this property, her hands were tied and
there was not the slightest hope for any large plan of
emancipation.

[8] Ibid., p. 126.

Dew's case was not as strong as it might appear at first glance. He denied the General Assembly the power to repeal acts of the colonial assembly and paid but slight regard to the power of abating nuisances. As we have shown slavery had no legal status until the colonial assembly gave it such in 1670. What was there to prevent its successor, the General Assembly, from repealing this and subsequent acts of the same nature? What, too, of the power to abate nuisances? No one denied that the legislature was competent to destroy other kinds of property regarded as dangerous. When the worthy legislators considered the militia and police bills they apparently thought slavery dangerous. Wherein lay the special feature that separated slavery and raised it above the power of the legislature?

One cannot agree with Dew in regard to the wisdom of inaction. It does not seem impossible that had some large plan for removing the free negroes and slaves surrendered for that purpose been adopted, a large diminution of the black population might have been effected. To declare that masters would not surrender their negroes in considerable numbers was to declare that masters so generous in spite of serious obstacles would become less active with the removal of these obstacles. Quite likely the whole of the black population would not be removed, but a large diminution could not but affect the State favorably.

Possessed of the largest slave interest of any State, possessed of one-fifth of the slave population in the United States, with a free black population exceeded only by that of Maryland, with a large fraction of her white population ready for abolition, Virginia's opportunity was great. Had some effectual scheme of abolition been adopted how greatly different might have been the history of the next hundred years. One cannot know whether the War for Southern Independence might have been averted, but it seems safe to assert that had Virginia not joined the Confederacy, the collapse of the latter would have been rapid.

Of one thing James McDowell had assured the legislators, that the slaveholding interest could never combine with any other but must stand alone. But alas, their money bags had become weights about their necks. On the one hand, the magnitude of the property involved precluded the possibility of any plan of abolition entailing compensation. On the other, their sacred respect for property rendered impossible every scheme that involved confiscation, whether partial or complete. Little matter that men, women, and children had perished and might do so again any day, slaves were property.

The General Assembly in its apathy, in its refusal to adopt any constructive program, clenched the grip of slavery on Virginia and made more certain her union with the States of the Confederacy and thus more terrible the tragedy of 1861.

APPENDIX

LIST OF DELEGATES TO THE CONVENTION

District of Amelia, Chesterfield, Cumberland, Nottoway, Powhatan, and Town of Petersburg.

John W. Jones, of Chesterfield.
Benjamin W. Leigh, of Chesterfield.
Samuel Taylor, of Chesterfield.
William B. Giles (Gov.), of Amelia.

District of Brunswick, Dinwiddie, Lunenburg, and Mecklenburg.

William H. Brodnax, of Dinwiddie.
George C. Dromgoole, of Brunswick.
Mark Alexander, of Mecklenburg.
William O. Goode, of Mecklenburg.

District of the City of Williamsburg, Charles City, Elizabeth City, James City, City of Richmond, Henrico, New Kent, Warwick, and York.

J. Marshall (C. J. U. S.), of Richmond.
Philip N. Nicholas, of Richmond City.
John Tyler, of Charles City.
John B. Clopton, of New Kent.

District of Shenandoah and Rockingham.

P. Harrison, of Rockingham.
J. Williamson, of Rockingham.
W. Anderson, of Shenandoah.
S. Coffman, of Shenandoah.

District of Augusta, Rockbridge, and Pendleton.

B. G. Baldwin, of Augusta.
Chapman Johnson, of Augusta.
William M'Coy, of Pendleton.
S. M'D. Moore, of Rockbridge.

District of Monroe, Greenbrier, Bath, Botetourt, Alleghany, Pocahontas, and Nicholas.

A. Beirne, of Monroe.
William Smith, of Greenbrier.
F. B. Miller, of Botetourt.
J. Baxter, of Pocahontas.

District of Sussex, Surry, Southampton, Isle of Wight, Prince George, and Greensville.

John Y. Mason, of Southampton.
J. Trezvant, of Southampton.
A. Claiborne, of Greensville.
John Urquhart, of Southampton.

District of Charlotte, Halifax, and Prince Edward.

John Randolph, of Charlotte.
William Leigh, of Halifax.
Richard Logan, of Halifax.
Richard N. Venable, of Prince Edward.

District of Spottsylvania, Louisa, Orange, and Madison.	James Madison (Ex-P), of Orange. Philip Barbour, of Orange. D. Watson,[1] of Louisa. Robert Stanard, of Spottsylvania.
District of Loudoun and Fairfax.	James Monroe [2] (Ex-P), of Loudoun. Charles F. Mercer, of Loudoun. Richard H. Henderson, of Loudoun. William H. Fitzhugh, of Fairfax.
District of Frederick and Jefferson.	John R. Cooke, of Frederick. Alfred H. Powell, of Frederick. Hierome L. Opie,[3] of Jefferson. Thomas Griggs, Jr., of Jefferson.
District of Hampshire, Hardy, Berkeley, and Morgan.	William Naylor, of Hampshire. W. Donaldson, of Hampshire. Elisha Boyd, of Berkeley. Philip C. Pendleton, of Berkeley.
District of Washington, Lee, Scott, Russell and Tazewell.	J. B. George, of Tazewell. A. M'Millan, of Lee. E. Campbell, of Washington. W. Byars, of Washington.
District of King William, King and Queen, Essex, Caroline, and Hanover.	John Roane, of King William. William P. Taylor, of Caroline. Richard Morris, of Hanover. J. M. Garnett, of Essex.
District of Wythe, Montgomery, Grayson, and Giles.	G. Cloyd, of Montgomery. H. Chapman, of Giles. J. P. Mathews, of Wythe. William Oglesby, of Grayson.
District of Kanawha, Mason, Cabell, Randolph, Harrison, Lewis, Wood, and Logan.	E. S. Duncan, of Harrison. J. Laidley, of Cabell. Lewis Summers, of Kanawha. Adam See, of Randolph.
District of Ohio, Tyler, Brooke, Monongalia, and Preston.	Philip Doddridge, of Brooke. Charles S. Morgan, of Monongalia. Alexander Campbell, of Brooke. E. M. Wilson, of Monongalia.

[1] David Watson, resigned, succeeded by Waller Holladay.
[2] James Monroe, resigned Dec. 12, succeeded by Joshua Osborne, Esq.
[3] H. L. Opie, resigned Dec. 16, succeeded by James M. Mason.

District of Fauquier and Culpeper.

John S. Barbour, of Culpeper.
John W. Green, of Culpeper.
John Scott, of Fauquier.
John Macrae,[4] of Fauquier.

District of Norfolk, Princess Anne, Nansemond, and Borough of Norfolk.

Littleton Tazewell, of Norfolk Borough.
Robert Taylor,[5] of Norfolk Borough.
George Loyall, of Norfolk Borough.
Joseph Prentis, of Nansemond.

District of Campbell, Buckingham and Bedford.

William Campbell, of Bedford.
Callohill Mennis,[6] of Bedford.
Samuel Claytor, of Campbell.
James Saunders, of Campbell.

District of Franklin, Patrick, Henry, and Pittsylvania.

George Townes, of Pittsylvania.
B. S. W. Cabell, of Pittsylvania.
Joseph Martin, of Henry.
A. Stuart, Jr., of Patrick.

District of Albemarle, Amherst, Nelson, Fluvanna, and Goochland.

James Pleasants, of Goochland.
William F. Gordon, of Albemarle.
L. P. Thompson, of Amherst.
Thomas Massie, Jr., of Nelson.

District of King George, Westmoreland, Lancaster, Northumberland, Richmond, Stafford, and Prince William.

William A. Dade,[7] of Prince William.
Ellyson Currie,[8] of Lancaster.
John Taliaferro,[9] of King George.
Fleming Bates, of Northumberland.

District of Matthews, Midlesex, Accomack, Northampton, and Gloucester.

T. R. Joynes, of Accomack.
T. M. Bayly, of Accomack.
Calvin H. Read,[10] of Northampton.
Abel P. Upshur, of Northampton.

---

[4] Macrae, resigned Jan. 3, succeeded by Thomas Marshall.
[5] Robert B. Taylor, resigned Nov. 7, succeeded by H. B. Grigsby.
[6] Mennis, resigned Nov. 26, succeeded by Samuel Branch.
[7] Dade, resigned Oct. 5, succeeded by Alexander Rose.
[8] Currie, died October 5, succeeded by Augustine Neale.
[9] Taliaferro, resigned Nov. 24, succeeded by John Coalter.
[10] Read, died October 6, succeeded by William K. Perrin.

LIST OF DELEGATES FOR THE SESSION OF 1831-32

Accomack ....Southey Grinalds
                                     John P. Drummond
Albemarle ....Rice W. Wood
                                     Thomas J. Randolph
Alleghany ....John Persinger
Amelia ....Richard Booker
Amherst ....Samuel M. Garland
Augusta ....John M'Cue
                                     Robert S. Brooke
Bath ....Andrew W. Cameron
Bedford ....Robert Campbell
                                     Edmund Pate
Berkeley ....Charles Faulkner
                                     William Good
Botetourt ....William Anderson
                                     George W. Wilson
Brooke ....John C. Campbell
Brunswick ....James H. Gholson
                                     John E. Shell
Buckingham ....William N. Patteson
                                     Philip A. Bolling
Cabell ....William Spurlock
Campbell ....William Rives
                                     William Daniel, Jr.
Caroline ....Charles Tod [1]
Charles City and New Kent.............James D. Halyburton
Charlotte ....John D. Richardson
Chesterfield ....William A. Patteson
Culpeper ....John S. Pendleton
                                     Edmund Broadus
Cumberland ....Allen Wilson
Dinwiddie ....William H. Brodnax
Elizabeth City and Warwick............Alexander W. Jones
Essex ....Archibald Ritchie
Fairfax ....Spencer M. Ball
Fauquier ....Marck A. Chilton
                                     Thomas Marshall

---

[1] William W. Dickinson in lieu of Charles Tod, who died during the session.

Fayette & Nicholas......................John G. Stephenson
Fluvanna ....George Stillman
Floyd ....Jacob Helms
Franklin ....Samuel Hale
                                    Wyley P. Woods
Frederick ....William Wood
                                    James G. Bryce
                                    John B. D. Smith
Giles ....William H. Snidow
Gloucester ....Thomas Smith
Goochland ....Archibald Bryce
Grayson ....Lewis Hail
Greenbrier ....Henry Erskine
Greensville ....Thomas Spencer
Halifax ....James C. Bruce
                                    William D. Sims
Hampshire ....Thomas Carskadon
                                    Ellias Poston
Hanover ....William H. Roane
Hardy ....John Mullen
Harrison ....George I. Williams
                                    William Johnson
Henrico ....John G. Wiliams [2]
Henry ....Peyton Gravely
Isle of Wight.........................James C. Jordan
James City ....⎫
York & Williamsburg...................⎬Robert Sheild
Jefferson ....John S. Callaher
                                    Henry Berry
Kanawha ....George W. Summers
King & Queen..........................Archibald R. Harwood
King George ....John Hooe
King William ....Benjamin F. Dabney
Lancaster & Richmond..................Robert W. Carter
Lee ....James Allen
Lewis ....Samuel L. Hays
Logan ....Anthony Lawson
Loudoun ....James M'Ilhaney
                                    Presley Cordell
                                    Samuel B. T. Caldwell

---

[2] Robert A. Mayo in lieu of Mr. Williams, declared ineligible.

Louisa .... Nicholas J. Poindexter
Lunenburg .... John T. Street
Madison .... Linn Banks [3]
Mathews & Middlesex.................. Houlder Hudgkins
Mason and Jackson...................... Nehemiah Smith
Mecklenburg .... William O. Goode
                                                         Alexander G. Knox
Monongalia .... Francis Billingsly
                                                         William G. Henry
Monroe .... John W. Kelly [4]
Montgomery .... William B. Preston
Morgan .... Henry A. Byrne [5]
Nansemond .... Richard D. Webb
Nelson .... Joseph C. Cabell
Norfolk County .... John A. Chandler
                                                         John P. Leigh
Northampton .... Miers W. Fisher
Northumberland .... Thomas H. Harvey
Nottoway .... Hezekiah R. Anderson
Ohio .... Samuel H. Fitzhugh
                                                         John Parriott
Orange .... Thomas Davis
Page .... William M. Robertson
Patrick .... Isaac Adams
Pendleton .... Harmon Hiner
Pittsylvania .... William Swanson
                                                         Vincent Witcher
Pocahontas .... John Gilliland
Powhatan .... Thomas Miller
Preston .... William Zinn
Prince Edward .... Asa Dupuy
Princess Anne .... Jeremiah T. Land
Prince George .... William Shands
Prince William .... Charles S. Carter
Randolph .... Joseph Hart
Rockbridge .... Samuel M'D. Moore
                                                         James M'Dowell
Rockingham .... William M'Mahon
                                                         Joseph Cline

---

[3] Linn Banks, Speaker.

[4] John J. Vawter in lieu of John W. Kelly declared unduly elected.

[5] Henry A. Byrne ejected, having no freehold.

Russell .... Archer Jessee
Scott .... Hiram Kilgore
Shenandoah .... Samuel Bare
William Carson
Southampton .... Jeremiah Cobb
Spottsylvania .... Robert D. Powell
Stafford .... Thomas G. Moncure
Surry .... John C. Crump
Sussex .... Jesse Hargrave
Tazewell .... Robert Gillespie
Tyler .... John M'Coy
Washington .... Thomas M'Cullock
John Keller
Westmoreland .... Willoughby Newton
Wood .... Isaac Morris
Wythe .... Charles L. Crockett
Norfolk Borough .... Miles King
Petersburg .... John T. Brown
Richmond City .... John Rutherfoord

List of Members of the Senate, 1831-32

Amelia, Powhattan, Chesterfield, and Town
   of Petersburg .... William Old
Bedford and Franklin...................... William Campbell
Spottsylvania, Caroline, and Essex........... Stafford H. Parker
Albemarle, Nelson and Amherst.............. Charles Cocke
Fauquier and Prince William................ Charles Hunton
Augusta and Rockridge..................... David W. Patteson
Shenandoah, Hardy, and Page............... Joel Pennybacker
Monongalia, Preston, and Randolph.......... Charles Morgan
Isle of Wight, Prince George, Southampton,
   Surry, and Sussex........................ Francis Rives
Halifax and Mecklenburg................... Nathaniel Alexander
Buckingham, Campbell, and Cumberland..... George Booker
Accomack, Northampton, Elizabeth City,
   York, Warwick, and Williamsburg......... John G. Joynes
Culpeper, Madison, and Orange............. Lawrence T. Dade
Frederick and Jefferson..................... Hierome Opie
Tazewell, Wythe, and Grayson.............. David M'Comas
Greenbrier, Monroe, Giles, Montgomery and
   Floyd .... Andrew Bierne

Charlotte, Lunenburg, Nottoway, and Prince
Edward ....Joseph Wyatt
Patrick, Henry, and Pittsylvania.............Ben. W. S. Cabell
Charles City, James City, New Kent, and
Henrico, and City of Richmond............Jacqueline B. Harvie
Stafford, King George, Westmoreland, Rich-
mond, Lancaster, and Northampton........William Basye
Rockingham and Pendleton..................Joseph Cravens
Berkeley, Morgan, and Hampshire............Elisha Boyd
Harrison, Lewis and Wood...................John M'Whorter
Washington, Russell, Scott and Lee..........George Cowen
Norfolk, Nansemond, Princess Anne, and
Borough of Norfolk.......................William Holt
(Speaker)
Brunswick, Dinwiddie, and Greensville........George Dromgoole
King & Queen, King William, Gloucester,
Mathews, and Middlesex...................William Armstead
Fluvanna, Goochland, Louisa, and Hanover...Horatio Winston
Loudoun and Fairfax........................William M'Carty
Alleghany, Bath, Pocahontas, and Botetourt...Charles Beale
Brooke, Ohio, and Tyler....................Jessie Edgington
Kanawha, Mason, Cabell, Logan, Nicholas,
Fayette, and Jackson......................William M'Comas

BIBLIOGRAPHY

MANUSCRIPTS

The unprinted manuscripts used in the preparation of this treatise are found in the archives of the Virginia State Library in six large classifications: Colonial Papers, Executive Communications, Executive Papers, the Executive Journal, the Governor's Letter Book, and Petitions to the General Assembly. Colonial Papers are arranged chronologically with folders for each year. They in turn are preserved in boxes plainly and adequately marked. Executive Communications and Executive Papers are respectively communications of the Governor to the General Assembly, and papers addressed to him by citizens. Kept in separate files, they too, are arranged chronologically, The Letter Book and the Executive Journal are bound volumes containing copies of letters sent out by the Governor and the minutes of the Governor's Council. In the first set volumes contain only the business of single years. Unfortunately the Letter Book for the year 1830-31 is lost. Petitions to the General Assembly are easy to use if one knows the approximate dates of those he wishes or the counties in which they originated. Though a few of the prayers are in print, the overwhelming part of these records down through the period treated in this paper are in manuscript.

OFFICIAL PUBLICATIONS

Acts Passed at a General Assembly of the Commonwealth of Virginia, I-CLX, CII not known to be extant in print or manuscript [Earl G. Swem, Bulletin of the Virginia State Library, X, 1079] (Williamsburg and Richmond, Va., 1776-   ).

Annual Reports of the Board of Directors of the Penitentiary with Accompanying Documents, [published annually after 1870, until 1866 in the House of Delegates journals but that year published separately for the first time, not until 1870 were they published separately and regularly] (Richmond, Va., 1870-   ).

Calendar of Virginia State Papers and Other Manuscripts, etc., 11 volumes, ed. by William P. Palmer (Richmond, Va., 1875-93).

Hening, William W., The Statutes at Large; Being a Collection of All the Laws of Virginia from the First Session of the Legislature in the Year 1619, etc., 13 vols. (Richmond, Va., 1819-23).

152   SLAVERY AGITATION IN VIRGINIA

Hotchkiss, Jedediah, Virginia: A Political and Geographical Summary, etc. (Richmond, Va., 1876).

Journal, Acts and Proceedings of a General Convention of the Commonwealth of Virginia Assembled in Richmond, etc. (Richmond, Va., 1829).

Journal of the House of Delegates of the Commonwealth of Virginia, I-CLX; X, XIII, XIV, XV, XXIII, XXXI, not known to be extant in print (Williamsburg and Richmond, Va., 1776-).

Journal of the Senate of the Commonwealth of Virginia, I-CLX; VIII-XV, XVII-XXV, XXVII, XXIX-XXXIV, XXXVII-XXXIX, XLII, XLVI, XLVIII, XLIX not known to be extant [Earl G. Swem] (Williamsburg and Richmond, 1776-).

Leigh, Benjamin W., The Revised Code of the Laws of Virginia, etc., 2 vols. (Richmond, Va., 1819).

Proceedings and Debates of the Virginia State Convention of 1829-30, etc. (Richmond, Va., 1830).

Shepherd, Samuel, The Statutes at Large of Virginia from October Session, 1792 to December Session, 1806, etc., 3 vols. (Richmond Va., 1835-36).

NEWSPAPERS AND PERIODICALS

Constitutional Whig, 1828-1832 (Richmond, Va., issues missing after Dec. 29, 1829, to Jan. 9, 1830).

Daily Richmond Whig, November 15, 1828–February 10, 1831 (Richmond, Va.).

The Genius of Universal Emancipation edited by Benjamin Lundy, 16 vols. (Washington, D. C., 1821-39, continued as Genius of Liberty).

National Intelligencer, 1831 (Washington, D. C.).

Nile's Weekly Register, 75 vols. (v. I-XII, XIII-XXIV) [New Series I-XII], XXV-XXXVI [3d. series I-XII], XXXVII-L [4th series I-XIV], LI-LXXIII [5th series I-XXIII], LXXIV-LXXV; Baltimore, 1811-37; Washington, 1837-39; Baltimore, 1839-48; Philadelphia, 1848-49. Publications suspended from March to June, 1848.

Richmond Commercial Compiler, 1829-1830 (Richmond, Va.).

Richmond Enquirer, 1828-1832 (Richmond, Va.).

CONTEMPORARY WRITINGS

Abolition of Negro Slavery. Debate in the Virginia Legislature of 1831-32 on the Abolition of Slavery, etc. (American Quarterly Review, XXII).

Address of the Board of Managers of the American Colonization Society to Its Auxiliary Societies (Washington, D. C., 1831).

The African Repository and Colonial Journal: 68 vols. (edited by R. R. Curley, Washington, D. C., 1826-92).

Andrews, E. A., Slavery and the Domestic Slave-Trade in the United States (Boston, Mass., 1836).

The Annual Reports of the American Society for Colonizing the Free People of Color, 93 vols. (Washington, D. C., 1818-1910).

Bourne, George, Picture of Slavery in the United States (Middletown, Conn., 1834).

Buckingham, J. S., The Slave States of America, 2 vols. (London and Paris).

Burnaby, Andrew, Burnaby's Travels in Virginia in 1759 (Virginia Historical Register and Literary Companion, V, nos. 1 and 2 Richmond, Va., 1852).

Coles, Edmund, Letters of Edward Coles (William and Mary College Quarterly, Series 2, VII).

Dew, Thomas R., Review of the Debate in the Virginia Legislature of 1831 and 1832 (Richmond, Va., 1832).

Douglass, Frederick, Narrative of the Life of Frederick Douglass, An American Slave, Written by Himself (Boston, 1845).

Floyd, John, Diary of John Floyd (John P. Branch Historical Papers of Randolph-Macon College, V, nos. 1 and 2).

Garrison, William L., Thoughts on African Colnization: or An Impartial Exhibition of the Doctrines, Principles and Purposes of The American Colonization Society, Together with the Resolutions, Addresses and Remonstrances of The Free People of Color (Boston, 1832).

Grey, Thomas, Confessions of Nat Turner, etc. (Richmond, Va., 1832).

Grigsby, Hugh B., Discourse on the Life and Character of Littleton W. Tazewell, etc. (Norfolk, Va., 1860).

———, The Virginia Convention of 1829-30, etc. (Richmond, Va., 1854).

Hall, Basil, Travels in North America in the Years 1827 and 1828, 3 vols. (Edinburgh, 1829).

Jefferson, Thomas, Notes on the State of Virginia (Philadelphia, 1794).

The Letter of Appomattox to the People of Virginia, etc. (Richmond, Va., 1832).

Martineau, Harriet, Society in America, 2 vols. (New York, 1837).

Monroe, James, The Writings of James Monroe, etc., 7 vols., edited by S. M. Hamilton (New York and London, 1898-1903).

Pleasants, Hugh R., Sketches of the Virginia Convention of 1829-30 (Southern Literary Messenger, XVII, Richmond, Va.).

Rankin, John, Letters on American Slavery: Addressed to Thomas Rankin (Newburyport, 2d ed., 1836).

Rogers, William B., The Virginia Convention, 1829. Letter of William B. Rogers to Henry (William and Mary College Quarterly, Series 2, vol. 7).

Slaughter, Philip, The Virginian History of African Colonization (Richmond, Va., 1855).

Smith, John, Captain J. Smith's Works, 1608-1631; ed. Edward Arber (Birmingham, England, 1884).

A South Carolinian, A Refutation of the Calumnies Circulated against the Southern and Western States, etc, (Charleston. S. C., 1822).

The Speech of Henry Berry (of Jefferson), In The House of Delegates of Virginia, On the Abolition of Slavery (Pamphlet published in Richmond, Va., 1832).

The Speeches of Philip A. Bolling in The House of Delegates of Virginia, On the Policy of the State in Relation to Her Colored Population: delivered on the 11th and 25th of January, 1832 published in Richmond, Va., 2d ed., 1832.

The Speech of William H. Brodnax (of Dinwiddie) in The House of Delegates of Virginia, On the Policy of the State with Respect to Its Colored Population (Pamphlet published in Richmond, 1832).

The Speech of John Thompson Brown in The House of Delegates of Virginia, On The Abolition of Slavery (Pamphlet published in Richmond, Va., 1832).

The Speech of John A. Chandler (of Norfolk County) in The House of Delegates of Virginia, On the Policy of the State with Respect to Her Slave Population (Pamphlet published in Richmond, Va., 1832).

The Speech of Charles Jas. Faulkner (of Berkeley) in The House of Delegates of Virginia, On the Policy of the State with Respect to Her Slave Population (Pamphlet published in Richmond, Va., 1832).

The Speech of James M'Dowell, Jr. (of Rockbridge) in The House of Delegates of Virginia, On the Slave Question: Delivered Saturday, January, 21, 1832 (Pamphlet published in Richmond, Va., 2d ed., 1832).

The Speech of Thomas Marshall (of Fauquier) in The House of Delegates On the Policy of the State in Relation to Her Colored Population: Delivered Saturday, January 14, 1832 (Pamphlet published in Richmond, Va., 2d. ed., 1832).

The Speech of Thomas Marshall in The House of Delegates of Virginia On the Abolition of Slavery: Delivered January 20, 1832 (American Quarterly Review, XXII).

The Speech of Thomas J. Randolph (of Albemarle) in the House of Delegates of Virginia, On The Abolition of Slavery: Delivered Saturday, Jan. 21, 1832 (Richmond, Va., 2d ed., 1832).

Tocqueville, Alexis de, Democracy in America, 2 vols. (translated, Henry Reeve, New York, 1898).

Tucker, St. George, A Dissertation on Slavery with A Proposal for the Gradual Abolition of It in the State of Virginia (Philadelphia, Penna., 1796).

A Virginian, Review of the Slave Question, etc. (Richmond, Va., 1833).

Williams, J., The South Vindicated. From the Treason and Fanaticism of the Northern Abolitionists (Philadelphia, 1836).

SECONDARY SOURCES

Adams, Alice D., The Neglected Period of Anti-Slavery in America, 1801-1831 (Boston, Mass., 1908).

Adams, Herbert B., The Life and Writings of Jared Sparks, 2 vols. (New York and Boston, 1893).

Ambler, Charles H., Life of John Floyd (John P. Branch Historical Papers of Randolph-Macon College, V, nos. 1 and 2, 1918).

——, Thomas Ritchie: A Study in Virginia Politics (Richmond, Va., 1913).

——, Sectionalism in Virginia from 1776-1861 (Chicago, 1910).

Anderson, Dice R., William Branch Giles: A Study in the Politics of Virginia and the Nation from 1790 to 1830 (Menasha, Wisconsin, 1914).

Ballagh, James C., A History of Slavery in Virginia (J. H. U. Studies, Extra Volume XXIV).

Bancroft, George, History of the United States from the Discovery of the American Continent, 5 vols. (Boston, 1852).

Bledsoe, Albert T., Liberty and Slavery, or Slavery in the Light of Moral and Political Philosophy, in Cotton is King and Pro-Slavery Arguments (ed., E. N. Elliott, Augusta, Ga., 1860).

Brown, Alexander, The First Republic in America, etc. (Boston and New York, 1898).

Bruce, Philip Alexander, Economic History of Virginia in the Seventeenth Century, etc., 2 vols. (New York and London, 1898).

A Century of Population Growth from the First Census of the United States to the Twelfth, 1790-1900 (Washington, 1909).

Chambers, William, Things as They Are in America (Philadelphia, 1854).

Collins, Winfield H., The Domestic Slave Trade (New York, 1904).

Dabney, Robert L., A Defence of Virginia (New York, 1867).

Drewry, William S., The Southampton Insurrection (Washington, D. C., 1890).

Fifty Years in Chains or The Life of an American Slave (New York, 1858).

Fox, Early Lee, The American Colonization Society, 1817-1840 (J. H. U. Studies, XXXVII).

Garrison, Wendell P., William Lloyd Garrison, 1805-1879. The Story of His Life as Told by His Children, 4 vols. (Boston and New York, 1909).

Gordon, Armistead C., William Fitzhugh Gordon, A Virginian of the Old School. His Life, Times, and Contemporaries (New York and Washington, 1909).

Goodell, William, The American Slave Code, in Theory and Practice: Its Distinctive Features Shown by Its Statutes, Judicial Decisions and Illustrative Facts (New York, 1853).

Harper, William, Slavery in the Light of Social Ethics, in Cotton Is King and Pro-Slavery Arguments (ed. E. N. Elliott, Augusta, Ga., 1860).

Levermore, George, An Historical Research Respecting the Opinions of the Founders of the Republic on Negroes as Slaves, as Citizens, and as Soldiers (Boston, 1863).

Locke, Mary S., Anti-Slavery in America from the Introduction of African Slaves to the Prohibition of the Slave Trade (Boston, 1901).

McGregor, James Clyde, The Disruption of Virginia (New York, 1922).

Munford, Virginia's Attitude toward Slavery and Secession (New York, 1909).

A Northern Man, The Planter, or Thirteen Years in the South (Philadelphia, 1853).

Olmstead, Frederick L., Journeys and Explorations in the Cotton Kingdom, 2 vols. (London, 1861).

Page, Thomas N., The Old South: Essays Social and Political (New York, 1892).

Phillips, Ulrich B., American Negro Slavery, A Survey of the Supply, Employment and Control of Negro Labor as Determined by the Plantation Régime (New York, 1918).

Redpath, James, The Public Life of Capt. John Brown, etc. (Boston, 1860).

Ruffin, Edmund, The Political Economy of Slavery, or The Institution Considered in Regard to Its Influence on Public Wealth and The General Welfare (Washington, 1857).

Russell, John H., The Free Negro in Virginia, 1619-1865 (J. H. U. Studies, XXXI).

Simms, William G., The Morals of Slavery, in the Pro-Slavery Argument as Maintained by the Most Distinguished Writers of the Southern States, etc. (Charleston, S. C., 1852).

Smith, Margaret V., Virginia, 1492-1892; a Brief Review of the Discovery of the Continent of North America with a History of the Executives, etc. (Washington, 1893).

Spears, John R., The American Slave Trade (New York, 1907).

The Suppressed Book about Slavery (New York, 1864).

Tyler, Lyon G., The Letters and Times of The Tylers, 3 vols. (Richmond, Va., 1884-1896).

Weston, George M., The Progress of Slavery in The United States (Washington, D. C., 1857).

Wilson, Henry, History of the Rise and Fall of the Slave Power in America, 3 vols. (Boston, 1872-77).

INDEX

Accomack, 113
Adams, Alice D., 13n.
African Centinel and Journal of
Liberty, 61
Alabama, 81
Alleghanies, 13, 34
Alexander, Mark, 43
Alexandria, Va., 12
Ambler, Charles H., 14, 62n.
American Colonization Society,
8n., 12, 13, 56, 102, 118n.
Anderson, Hezekiah R., 27n., 44,
67n., 148
Appomattox, 134
Augusta, 25. *See also* Petitions

Baldwin, B. G., 16, 44
Banks, Linn, 67, 148
Barbour, John S., 43, 145
Barbour, Philip P., 24, president
of convention, 40, 43, 144
Bates, Fleming, 43, 145
Baxter, J., 27n., 44
Bayly, T. M., 43, 145
Beirne, A., 27n., 44
Blunt, 61, 123n.
Bolling, Philip A., 84, 106, 146
Booker, George, 110, 149
Boyd, Elisha, 44
Branch, Samuel, 43
Brodnax, William H., 12, 25, 27,
43, 67n.; defends property, 79,
81; advises removal of free
blacks, 82; reports, 83, 88, 90,
95, 96, 98; demands powers of
coercion, 99, 100; reports sub-
stitute bill, 102, 104, 105, 106,
107, 117, 124, 128, 132, 143, 146
Brown, Hack, 61n.
Brown, John, 60, 61n.
Brown, J. Thompson, 67n., 74, 84,
85, 86, 87, 106, 107, 149
Brunswick, 77
Bryce, Archibald, 67n., 83, 93, 100,
104, 106, 147
Buckingham, 119, 123
Burgesses, House of, 1
Byars, W., 27n., 44

Cabell, B. S. W., 43, 145
Campbell, Alexander, 44, 144

Campbell, E., 44, 144
Campbell, John C., 67n., 91, 98,
100, 105, 106, 107, 146
Campbell, William, 27n., 43, 145
Carter, Charles S., 73, 97, 128, 148
Central Board of Commissioners,
102, 104, 107, 108
Chandler, John, 67n., 74, 84, 85,
100, 131, 148
Chapman, H., 27n., 44, 144
Charles City, 72n., 119. *See also*
Petitions
Charleston, W. Va., 12
Claiborne, A., 43, 143
Clay, Henry, 12, 56
Claytor, Samuel, 44, 145
Clements, Isham W., 49
Clopton, John B., 27n., 43, 143
Cloyd, G., 44, 144
Coalter, John, 43, 145
Cobb, Jeremiah, 67n., 149
Coffman, S., 44, 143
College of William and Mary, 135
Collins, Winfield H., 92n.
Colonization, impossible, 138
Committee of Courts of Justice,
124
Committee of General Laws, re-
ceives removal bill, 109
Committee on the Coloured
Population, 67; report of, 83;
report accepted, 94; reports re-
moval bill, 95
Confederacy, 142
Connecticut, 81
Constitution of 1830, adoption of,
45
Convention, act to organize, 22
Cooke, John R., 27, 29, 30, 32, 42,
43, 144
Culpeper, 119. *See also* Petitions

Daniel, William, 67n., 106, 146
Delaware, 13
De Tocqueville, 9n.
Dew, Thomas R., 59, 135, 136, 137,
139, 140, 141
Digest of the Laws, Customs,
Manners, and Institutions of
Ancient and Modern Nations,
a, 135

159

162 INDEX